The Bike to Work Guide

Save Gas • Go Green • Get Fit

RONI SARIG WITH PAUL DORN

Aadamsmedia

AVON, MASSACHUSETTS

ISBN 10: 1-60550-633-8
ISBN 13: 978-1-60550-633-3

Published by
Adams Media, an F+W Media Company
57 Littlefield Street, Avon, MA 02322. U.S.A.
www.adamsmedia.com

Contains material adapted and abridged from *The
Everything® Bicycle Book*, by Roni Sarig, copyright
© 1998 by F+W Publications, Inc., ISBN 10:
1-55850-706-X, ISBN 13: 978-1-55850-706-7.

Printed in Canada.

J I H G F E D C B A

Library of Congress Cataloging-in-Publication Data
is available from the publisher.

This publication is designed to provide accurate and
authoritative information with regard to the subject
matter covered. It is sold with the understanding that the
publisher is not engaged in rendering legal, accounting,
or other professional advice. If legal advice or other
expert assistance is required, the services of a competent
professional person should be sought.

  —From a *Declaration of Principles* jointly adopted by
  a Committee of the American Bar Association and a
  Committee of Publishers and Associations

Many of the designations used by manufacturers and
sellers to distinguish their product are claimed as
trademarks. Where those designations appear in this book
and Adams Media was aware of a trademark claim, the
designations have been printed with initial capital letters.

The pages of this book are printed on 100% post-consumer
recycled paper.

This book is available at quantity discounts
for bulk purchases. For information, please
call 1-800-289-0963.

ACKNOWLEDGMENTS
I would like to thank Chelsea King,
of Adams Media, for providing the
opportunity to develop this book.

I would like to thank the bicyclists of San
Francisco, especially those involved with
the San Francisco Bicycle Coalition and
Critical Mass, for fostering my recovery
of bicycling as an adult; the bicycling
community of Davis, California, long an
inspiration to bicyclists across the United
States; and the bicyclists of Sacramento,
California, a truly wonderful and
underappreciated bicycling city.

I would also like to acknowledge my wife,
Marianne Skoczek, always a source of
intelligent inspiration.

         —Paul Dorn

CONTENTS

CHAPTER 1

Why Commute by Bicycle

There are many great reasons to travel to work by bicycle. These include enhanced health, saving the environment, saving money, and saving time. But the greatest appeal of bicycle commuting is simply that it's fun. And who couldn't use more fun in their lives?

Does anyone have an enjoyable commute? Certainly not motorists, sitting in parking lots disguised as "free" ways. Not transit users, crammed into packed buses or trains. Bicycle commuters have fun. From conversations and surveys over many years with bicycle commuters across the United States, we know that "joy" is a major motivation. People might *start* commuting by bike to improve their fitness or save money or out of a desire for sustainability, but they *persist* as bicycle commuters because it is fun.

Ask motorists about their commute, and they'll talk about road rage, a horrific crash they observed, traffic congestion, high gas prices, expensive repairs, parking tickets, and fights with insurance adjusters. Ask transit riders about their commute, and they might talk about missed connections, stale air on the bus or subway, and loud or obnoxious fellow passengers. Ask bicyclists about their commute, and they will smile. And likely mention the endorphin rush, the fresh air, the wildlife they may have seen that morning, a new coffee shop discovery, or how quickly their 401(k) accounts are swelling with money saved not driving.

Bicycle commuting is fun.

HEALTH BENEFITS

The United States confronts a growing public health crisis. The Centers for Disease Control and Prevention (CDC) reports that in the past thirty years, the percentage of overweight and obese adults (aged 20–74) has increased to nearly 33 percent. Excessive weight contributes to many diseases and health conditions, including hypertension (high blood pressure), osteoarthritis, type 2 diabetes, coronary heart disease, stroke, and certain cancers.

There are clear physical health benefits of bicycle commuting. The CDC recommends that adults engage in moderate-intensity physical activities for at least thirty minutes at least five days a week. Such activity is easily accomplished by bike commuting everyday.

A less stressful commute also contributes to mental well-being. In recent years, researchers have confirmed the value of regular exercise not only for physical health, but also for reducing anxiety and depression. A four-month research study at Duke University of people suffering from depression found that 60 percent of the participants overcame their depression by exercising for thirty minutes three times a week without antidepressant medication—the same percentage rate as for those who treated their depression only with medication.

Of course, there are other ways to get exercise. You might join a gym, hire a personal trainer, develop a fitness regimen, install exercise equipment in the basement, and dedicate portions of your week to regular workouts. That works. But is it fun? Some might enjoy riding a stationary bike in a gym. But with pressing work, family, and life obligations, most people eventually lose the motivation to continue with tedious gym activity.

Bicycle commuting improves physical and mental health.

ENVIRONMENTAL BENEFITS

Sustainability is a rapidly emerging priority in the United States. There is increasing awareness and concern about global climate change, international demand for energy, loss of natural habitat to sprawl, health issues related to air quality, challenges with water provision, and destructive agricultural practices.

Policymakers are struggling to find solutions to promote environmental and economic sustainability. Many enlightened politicians, especially at the local level, are embracing bicycling as an important component of an environment-friendly transportation system. In recent years, many cities across the United States have added miles of bike lanes and bike paths, added bike racks to buses and trains, created bike parking facilities, and funded bicycle-safety education programs. This has made bicycle commuting more attractive, and there is evidence that more people are biking. Much more work remains to be done.

Many individuals are also changing their personal consumption habits. They are recycling, replacing incandescent bulbs with energy-efficient compact fluorescents, buying organic foods, using energy-efficient appliances, acquiring fuel-efficient cars, and installing solar panels. But are any of these necessary activities fun?

The bicycle is the most energy-efficient personal transportation device ever created. Bicycle commuting is sustainable—and fun.

ECONOMIC BENEFITS

Life has gotten expensive. Housing, food, movies, health care, and college tuition are all more expensive. Retirement is more challenging. And gas prices have risen significantly. While many debate "peak oil"—the idea that the world has already used half of all oil, meaning a future of diminishing fuel supplies—the days of $3-a-gallon gas are far, far behind.

According to the American Automobile Association, the average annual cost of operating a small sedan for 15,000 miles totals $7,871. Larger vehicles cost $9,380 per year. Vehicle costs include depreciation, finance charges, fuel, maintenance, tires, tolls, insurance, and taxes. According to the Census Bureau, the median annual household income in the United States in 2006 was $48,201, meaning the cost of car ownership is 15–20 percent of the typical household's income. In other words, Americans spend the first ten weeks of each year working to pay for their car.

People are struggling to cope with this economic challenge. They are using credit cards more, eating out less often, working longer hours, staying home for vacation, postponing retirement, shopping for bargains, and clipping coupons. But is any of this fun?

Bicycles are affordable. A quality bicycle can be bought for the cost of about one car payment, will never need fueling, and is cheaply repaired.

Bicycle commuting is affordable, and fun.

TIME EFFICIENCY

Not only is life expensive, life is busy. Raising kids, working a job or two, buying necessities, and keeping a home all demand more and more time. We are always looking to squeeze more time out of our week. Yet for the most part, we continue to drive.

Bicycle commuting is efficient. It saves time. According to the Federal Highway Administration, nearly half of all trips in the United States are three miles or less. More than one-quarter of all trips are less than a mile. A three-mile trip takes about twenty minutes by bicycle. In a busy city, traveling three miles in a car can take longer. Just getting a car started, out of a parking space, into traffic, through lights and congestion, and parked again after possibly circling several times seeking a space can take far longer. For many trips, bicycles are simply faster point to point.

Bicycle commuting also saves you a trip to the local gym. It saves time you might otherwise spend at the gas station, the oil-change shop, the car wash, the traffic court, or the Department of Motor Vehicles. And given that the average American works ten weeks a year just to pay car bills, bicycle commuting might save you the necessity of keeping that second job.

And bicycle commuting is always more fun than sitting in traffic.

BICYCLES IN CONTEMPORARY TRANSPORTATION

Many in the developed world attempt to dismiss bicycles as an archaic method of transportation, from the era of the sailing vessel and horse cart. These skeptics would suggest the automobile has made the bicycle obsolete. But the bicycle and automobile aren't respective stages of transportation evolution, they are contemporaries. The car and the bike have co-evolved, continuing to develop and advance in tandem.

Even today, across the world, more trips are made by bicycle than by automobile. In the year 2007, global bike manufacturers produced more than 130 million bicycles, more than doubling total global automobile production of

57 million. The Earth Policy Institute reported in 2008 that overall, since 1970, bicycle output has nearly quadrupled, while car production has merely doubled. Even in the United States, bicycle sales exceed car sales each year (though many of those bikes are children's models).

When you commute by bicycle, you are not just relating in a direct way to your immediate community; you are traveling the way most of the world's population travels.

The future looks brighter than ever for bicycling. Concerns about the ecological and economic impacts of automobiles, the diminishing availability and increasing cost of petroleum, challenges with public health, and frustration with pervasive traffic congestion have resulted in a new interest in bicycling for transportation.

Many countries in Northern Europe—notably Holland, Denmark, and Germany—have aggressively pursued bike-friendly public policies, creating new bike paths and lanes, enhancing transit access for bicyclists, adding bike parking facilities, and even closing sections of major cities to auto traffic.

In 2007, Paris introduced an innovative bike-sharing program, Paris Vélib' (Vélo Liberté), which placed thousands of bikes at hundreds of locations around the city that people can use at low cost for short-distance trips with an electronic smart card. Aided by a transit strike shortly after the program's launch, Paris Vélib' has been a phenomenal success, used for 3.7 million trips in its first two months. By the end of 2007, Parisians could find 1,451 Vélib'stations and 20,600 bikes at locations across the city. The Paris experiment has since been replicated in several other European cities, and a similar SmartBike program was launched in 2008 in Washington, DC.

In the United States, bicycling is gaining strength as cities struggle to cope with expensive energy, noxious traffic, and strapped public budgets. The city of Portland, Oregon, has built hundreds of miles of bike lanes and paths, and bicyclists are now more than 5 percent of all commuters. (Nationally, approximately 1 percent of commuters are bicyclists.) New York City has seen a doubling in bike commuters, as the city improves the streets for bicycling. Other cities, including San Francisco, Chicago, Minneapolis, and Seattle, have also seen significant growth in bicycle commuters this decade.

American bicycle racer Lance Armstrong's success in the Tour de France in the late 1990s through early 2000s raised the visibility of bicycling in the United States. Armstrong has also become a strong proponent of bicycle commuting, opening a bike shop in 2008 called Mellow Johnny's (a play on the Tour de France's leader jersey, or *maillot jaune*) in downtown Austin, which promotes bicycle commuting and features showers, lockers, and bike parking facilities for commuters.

Bicyclists are also emerging as a political force. The League of American Bicyclists continues to advocate successfully in Washington, DC, for bike-friendly policies and funding, attracting more than 500 activists to the nation's capital for the 2008 National Bike Summit. The Thunderhead Alliance, a national coalition of state and local bicycle advocacy organizations, now has more than 150 member groups in all fifty states. Bicyclists have mobilized in Critical Mass events in cities around the world, raising awareness of bicycling and confronting the dominance of automobiles.

The American bicycle industry is recognizing the growth potential of the commuting bike market. Mountain bike pioneer Joe Breeze dedicated his company, Breezer Bikes, exclusively to the commuter bike market in 2002. Other bike makers have also developed commuting-specific models, responding to consumer demand.

In the first decade of the new millennium, the bicycle is firmly entrenched as a permanent fixture in global transportation. And the future looks bright.

THE GOAL OF THIS BOOK

Millions of Americans already ride bicycles. According to the United States Department of Transportation National Survey of Pedestrian and Bicyclist Attitudes and Behaviors, in 2002 approximately 57 million people, or 27.3 percent of the adult population, rode a bicycle at least once during the summer. Many people already bicycle for fitness, recreation, and fun.

A goal of this book is to help these people extend the fun they have bicycling on weekends to their daily commute. This book will also be helpful to people that haven't bicycled since they were teenagers but are seeking an escape from high fuel and car costs. This book will help those looking for an alternative to gas-pump piracy. And this book will also help those people who want more joy in their lives.

CHAPTER 2

Bicycle Technology

The bicycle happens to be the most efficient form of transportation created. Though there are many styles of bikes—including racing, touring, and mountain—all share certain design characteristics and parts.

MAIN PARTS OF THE BICYCLE

While there are many types and styles of bicycles, the basic structure and what makes them go is the same. Let's take a close look at the makeup of this incredible machine.

THE FRAME: THE HEART OF THE BIKE

The bike frame is generally what we talk about when we talk about the bike. Bike manufacturers are generally in the business of making frames; component manufacturers—such as Shimano, SRAM, and Campagnolo—make the rest of the parts and sell them to bike manufacturers. While the frame is not necessarily the most expensive part of the bike, it is the most important. A good bike design begins with (and practically ends with) the frame.

the frame

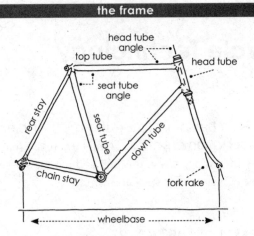

FRAME GEOMETRY

The tubing on most conventional bike frames is designed to form a diamond shape. This arrangement goes back at least 100 years to the earliest safety bicycles and hasn't changed much since. The diamond frame's nearly triangular shape (made by the seat, top, head, and down tubes) provides strength—because the triangle is the sturdiest shape for construction.

The top tube, across the top of the bike, connects the seat area to the steering area. Usually, the top tube runs roughly parallel to the ground, though on step-through bicycles (often mistakenly called "women's bikes") the top tube slopes up from lower on the seat tube. Step-through bicycles are popular with bicycle commuters who might wear skirts, or with those who because of age or other infirmity find it difficult to raise a leg over the top tube.

The head tube is located just above the front wheel and below the handlebars. It connects the steering system to the front fork, which holds the front wheel. The down tube extends diagonally down from the bottom of the head tube to the bottom bracket (the intersection of the seat tube and the down tube), which is where the crankset (chainwheel, crank, and pedals) is based. The seat tube connects the bottom bracket to the top tube.

In addition to the four main tubes, which give the bike its diamond-shaped bone structure, the frame consists of two pairs of thinner tubes. Two seat stays connect the point just below the seat, where the seat tube and the top tube meet, to the two sides of the rear axle. Two chain stays connect the same points on the rear axle to the bottom bracket. The area where the seat and chain stays meet at the rear-wheel axle is called the dropout. The seat stay, chain stay, and seat tube form a section of the frame known as the rear triangle.

The subtle but important variations in frame design come in the area known as frame geometry—how the angles and lengths of the tubes relate to each other. Though all bikes may appear similar in shape, very slight differences in the angles of the tubes can make huge differences in the comfort and performance of the bike.

FRAME SIZE

The size of a bicycle frame can be measured in inches or centimeters. The measure is typically the length of the seat tube, from the center of the bottom bracket to the top of the seat lug. However, some bike companies (usually foreign companies) measure frame size as the length of the seat tube from the center of the bottom bracket to the center of the top tube. The difference between the two styles of measuring will be about ½", which is a lot in the precision world of cycling design, so make sure you know how size is being measured.

The most desirable characteristics in bike parts are lightweight and strength. Materials should also be sufficiently rigid, meaning they'll keep their shape and won't give way under stress, and noncorrosive. While a flexible bike is valued by most riders, suspension should be provided through design (or through the use of shock absorbers and tires), not through the frame material.

BICYCLE FRAME MATERIALS

For more than a century, steel was the standard material in the manufacture of bike frames, but today most frames are aluminum, and many other higher-end bikes are made with lighter-weight carbon fiber and composites, and titanium. Depending on who you are and what your normal ride is like, talk to a representative from your local bike store to determine which choice of bicycle frame material is right for your commuting needs.

BIKE COMPONENTS

Now let's break apart the rest of the bike and see what makes it run.

THE SEAT

The bike seat or saddle is attached to the seat post, which extends out of the seat tube above the top tube.

THE STEERING SYSTEM

The steering system is made of a few parts held together in the head tube. The stem extends out above the head tube and typically bends outward to hold the handlebars.

THE WHEELS

While wheels vary considerably in weight and size depending on the type of bike, all bicycle wheels have a hub at the center where the wheel axle is located. The axle connects to the bike frame in the front by means of the fork (at the fork ends) and in the back by the seat stay and chain stay.

THE DRIVETRAIN

The drivetrain starts with the pedals, which is where the power source (the rider) meets the locomotive mechanism. The pedals are held in place by the cranks, which are strong bars that jut out of the chainwheel. The chainwheel is the set of circular gears, or sprockets (on the right side of the frame).

At its center, called the crank spindle, the chainwheel connects to the bottom bracket of the bike and turns by means of ball bearings. The chain runs around the sprockets of the chainwheel and connects around the back wheel's axle at the freewheel, or cassette, which has sprockets of its own, called cogs. The freewheel, or cassette, attaches to the back wheel's hub, turning the back wheel whenever the chain moves—which in turn makes the bike move.

the drivetrain

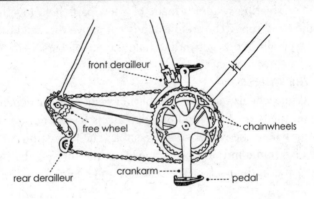

front derailleur

free wheel · · · · · · · · · · · · · · · · chainwheels

rear derailleur   crankarm · · · · · ·   · · · · · · · pedal

THE GEARS

Most bikes have a gear system that allows riders to adjust pedaling difficulty by moving the bike chain onto larger or smaller sprockets. Gears on most bicycles are operated by mechanisms called derailleurs; some bicycles use an internal hub to change gears. Derailleurs move the chain sideways onto the desired sprocket wheel. They are activated by gear levers, which are shifted by hand, located most frequently on the handlebars, generally incorporated with the brake levers.

THE BRAKES

Brakes are operated by brake levers located on the handlebars. The brake levers connect to brake cables that extend to the brakes near the top of the front and rear wheels (rim brakes) or to a disc mounted on the hub (disc brakes). Some bicycles use drum brakes operated by levers, or a coaster brake that enables the rider to stop the bike by pressing backward on the pedals.

BALL BEARINGS

Though hidden from sight, tiny ball bearings are used in bicycles and play a crucial role in how bicycles operate. In fact, bicycles and ball bearings go way back. Those little hard steel spheres, used in countless applications throughout this century, were first invented for use in the bicycle back in the mid-1800s.

Ball bearings are used in the hubs of the wheels as an interface between fixed parts (the axles) and moving parts (the wheels). Because ball bearings significantly reduce the road resistance exerted on a bike and the friction between wheels and frame, these tiny metal balls play a larger role than any other bike part in making the bicycle an efficient vehicle.

In addition to their use in the wheels, ball bearings are used in the head tube to facilitate steering, in the crankset to allow the chainwheels to spin while they're held by the bottom bracket, and in the pedals to allow rotation around the pedal axle. So that ball bearings generate the least amount of friction and resistance, grease is used as a lubricant between the balls and the rolling surface.

THE HEADSET

The headset uses ball bearings to enable steering. The handlebar stem locks into the head tube at the upper headset and connects with the fork shaft, or steer tube, inside the head tube. The fork shaft then exits the head tube at the lower headset, splits, and extends down to connect to the front wheel. While the head tube remains fixed, the steering system turns due to the ball bearings in both the upper and lower headsets.

STEERING

Built into the design of a bike are the angles and arrangements of the steering system, known as the steering geometry. The steering geometry determines how well a bicycle will handle—that is, how accurate and easy to maneuver steering will be. This is best indicated by a measurement called the trail.

The trail is the measure of the distance between the front wheel's point of contact with the road and the point where the steering axis, if extended beyond the head tube and fork, would touch the ground. In general, as the trail becomes larger, the bike becomes more stable but less responsive in steering.

The fork rake and the head-tube angle determine the trail. The rake is the amount the fork slopes forward. It is measured as the distance between the line extended to the ground from the steering axis and a parallel line extending to the ground from the wheel axle. The larger the rake, the smaller the trail. So as rake increases, the bike becomes less stable and more responsive.

The head-tube angle is another variable that affects trail. As long as the rake stays the same, a steeper head-tube angle will make the trail smaller, while a shallower angle will make it larger. Thus, shallow angles encourage stability while steep angles bring more steering response.

To some extent, wheel size affects trail as well. While most wheels are large enough to leave a sufficiently large trail no matter what the rake, bikes with very small wheels (children's bikes, some folding bikes) should have small rakes to maintain the trail, and, thus, stability.

WHEELS AND TIRES

A bicycle wheel is made up of a rim, spokes, and a hub, with a tire and inner tube secured to the rim. The bike wheel, which is light and yet supports heavy loads, is quite an engineering marvel. However, both wheels of a bike need to be perfectly true (flat and unwarped) and aligned to maintain balance and efficient handling.

THE HUB

The hub is located at the center of the wheel and surrounds the wheel's axle. While the axle is fixed and bolted to the bike frame (at the dropouts, or fork ends), the hub turns the wheel around the axle through the use of ball bearings. At the sides of the hub, just inside of where the axle connects to the frame, hub flanges flare out to form flat disc surfaces that contain holes for the spokes.

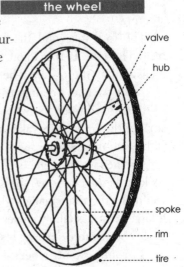

the wheel

valve

hub

spoke

rim

tire

SPOKES

Spokes are needed on a wheel to connect the rim to the hub, to provide support for the wheel, and to absorb forces (of both the road and the rider) exerted on the wheel. However, unlike the spokes of a wagon wheel, bicycle spokes hold the wheel together through tension (by pulling in the rim), not through compression (holding the rim in place). Tighter spokes make for stronger wheels.

Spokes are made of stainless steel and have nipple heads at the end for attaching to the rim and tightening. At the hub, spokes attach to one of the hub flanges, alternating between right and left sides. Wheels may have radial spokes, tangent or crossed spokes, or a combination of the two. Radial spokes simply connect a point on the rim to a point on the hub and do not cross each other, while the stronger tangential spokes wrap around the hub and connect to two points on the rim, crossing other spokes in the process. Most bicycle wheels have 20–36 spokes.

Some aerodynamic wheels used for racing do not use traditional stainless steel wire spokes. Instead, they may have 2–8 blades made of a composite material. Or, wheels may be solid discs with no spokes at all. While these aero wheels have less wind resistance, they are heavier and more difficult to make true if bent.

THE RIM

Rims are most often made of aluminum. Higher-end rims used for racing are made with carbon fiber. Rims are generally flat on the inside with a concave groove, or tire bed, on the outside. The rim is lined with holes the spokes run through. The spokes are fastened by tightening nipples. Spokes will often become loose, causing the wheel to come out of true. This is easy to remedy with a special spoke wrench, tightening nipples so each spoke in the wheel is at equal tension.

TIRES

Most bicycle tires are clinchers, which have metal or Kevlar wires along the edges that hook into a deep-bedded rim. A tire is made of several layers of fabric, reinforced with a puncture-resistant Kevlar layer or threads, which is then coated with rubber and shaped with a tread design. A separate inner tube, usually made of synthetic rubber, fits inside the tire.

Tires, of course, need to be properly inflated to work. Higher-pressure tires generate less resistance against the ground and roll faster. For suspension purposes, though, lower-pressure tires provide a smoother ride. In addition, an effective tread pattern makes tires more stable on the ground and less likely to skid. While some racing bikes reduce friction by having no tread at all, off-road bikes perform better with large treads that grip the ground.

TRANSMISSION

Transmission refers to the parts of the bike that make it go. Besides your own feet, the transmission includes the bike's drivetrain and the gear system.

THE CRANKSET AND PEDALS

The crankset consists of the chainwheels, which revolve around the bottom bracket by means of a spindle, and the cranks, which are the arms that turn the chainwheels. Pedals are attached to the cranks. The bottom bracket spindle uses ball bearings to turn the crankset in the fixed bottom bracket. Most bikes with variable gears have two or three chainwheels (a double or triple crankset). The chainwheels, or chainrings, are located on the right side of the bike (attached to the right crank) and increase in size as they move away from the bike. Each chainwheel has teeth on which the chain is threaded. As riders switch gears, the chain moves from one chainwheel to another. Larger chainwheels are responsible for the high gears that are difficult to pedal and that move the bike fast, while smaller chainwheels engage the low gears used to climb hills.

Crankarms, or simply cranks, attach to the bottom bracket spindle. They are fairly standard, with slight variations in length (160–180 mm) and design. Most cranks are suitable as long as they contribute to a rider's proper bike fit (along with frame size and seat height), are strong enough to withstand pedaling force (which is exerted on the crank-spindle connection), and turn the chainwheels effectively. However, slightly longer crankarms will give the rider more leverage in climbing hills and more pedal power on level ground. There is a limit to how long crankarms can be, though. They must be short enough to allow ample clearance between the pedals and the ground at all times.

Crankarm ends attach to the pedals at the pedal axle, the midpoint on the inside of the pedals. Pedals rotate around the pedal axle through the use of ball bearings. The movements of the pedal independent to the crankarms enables riders to keep their feet planted on the pedals throughout the 360-degree pedal stroke and to get the proper leverage for maximum pedaling efficiency. A few different types of pedals are commonly found on bicycles. The ordinary flat pedals come in a variety of shapes and degrees of traction. Many pedals used for higher performance bicycling are called clipless, which require special shoes with cleats attached to the sole that clamp into the pedal. Clipless pedals improve pedaling efficiency by holding the feet on the pedal to provide more stability and power in the pedaling upstroke. Most cleats used with clipless pedals detach easily when a bicyclist needs to slow or stop, usually by moving the heel of the foot away from the pedal.

THE CHAIN

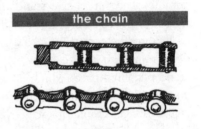

the chain

Chain design is standard in almost all bikes and has remained largely unchanged for many years. Some higher-performance chains intended for racing have become more narrow, and require special cranksets and cassettes. The tooth-and-link chain is made of two parallel sets of steel-link plates with cylindrical rollers between them at the joints. The teeth of the chainwheels and rear cogs thread into the space between the rollers. A light lubricant is needed

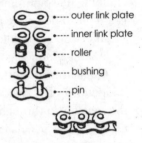

•---- outer link plate
•---- inner link plate
•---- roller
•---- bushing
•---- pin

to keep the chain lubricated and running smoothly, and the chain should be kept free of grime, dirt, and rust.

For the chain to run properly, chainwheels and cogs should be directly in line and centered. Gear settings that require the chain to deviate most (for example, a setting that uses the outermost chainwheel and the innermost cog) cause more wear on the chain and decreased pedaling efficiency. A chain tool is used to disconnect the chain from the drivetrain, by pushing out an individual pin from a joint. Some chains can be "broken" and reattached with special chain links.

FREEWHEEL AND COGS

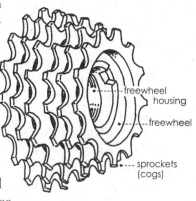

the freewheel and cogs

Most bicycles come with rear cassettes, with the free-wheel mechanism incorporated into the rear hub. The freewheel is the mechanism attached to the rear axle that allows (with the help of ball bearings) the rear wheel to turn without the rider having to pedal (known as coasting). Coasting is accomplished when levers, or pawls, in the free-wheel that work to engage the wheel during pedaling will disengage (causing that familiar clicking sound that you hear) during coasting.

freewheel housing

freewheel

sprockets (cogs)

Usually installed around the freewheel are a series of cogs, or sprockets, similar in appearance to the chainwheels on the crankset, but smaller in size and more numerous (typically there are 7–8 of them, while higher-performance bicycles may have 9–10 cogs). Like chainwheels, cogs are located on the right side of the wheel and progress in size, though cogs get smaller as they move away from the rear wheel. The chain, which is threaded onto the chainwheel in front, wraps around the teeth of a cog in the rear. As riders switch gears, the chain moves from one cog to another. Unlike the chainwheels (which work in the opposite way), the larger cogs make your pedaling easier, while the smaller ones give you more power.

GEARS

The gear of a bicycle simply refers to the position of the chain. It will always be threaded on one (of the 2–3) chainwheels in front and one (of the 7–8) cogs in the rear. The number of gears or speeds a bike has is equal to the number of possible combinations of chainwheel and cog settings. It can be determined by multiplying the number of cogs by the number of chainwheels. For instance, a bike with eight cogs and three chainwheels will have twenty-four gears or speeds.

While the sizes of gears increase relative to each other, the measurable size of chainwheels and cogs—and the range between the gears—vary from bike to bike. Some bikes have extra small gears designed for hill climbing, while other bikes lack smaller gears. Because the teeth on cogs and chainwheels are of a standard size in order to fit with standard chains, the size of a cog or chainwheel is often measured by the number of teeth it has. For instance, a 40T cog will have forty teeth.

Difficulty in pedaling, however, is not a matter of the individual sizes of the cog and chainwheel used, but rather of the ratio of the two together. That is, the combined size of a midsized cog and chainwheel may be equal to the combined size of a small cog and large chainwheel, but the two settings will not provide equal difficulty in pedaling because the gear ratio of the latter is much greater than the former (and therefore makes the bicycle more difficult to pedal).

DERAILLEURS AND SHIFT LEVERS

Shift levers located on the handlebars regulate the switching of gears. Most bicycles have two levers—one that moves the chain between the chainwheels in front (typically the left lever) and one that moves the chain between the cogs in back (typically the right lever). The levers connect to the derailleurs, which physically shift the gears through flexible cables that run along the bike frame.

The rear derailleur is typically attached to the dropout (near the rear wheel axle) with a pivot bolt that allows it to move lengthwise along the rear drivetrain. Most rear derailleurs have two chain-guide wheels through which the chain is threaded. Moving the gear levers causes the cables to be pulled or released, thus either pulling the derailleur in toward the wheel or allowing it to move farther away from the wheel. As the derailleur moves, it takes the chain with it, causing the chain to move to a larger or smaller cog—thus switching gears.

the rear derailleur (left) and front derailleur (right)

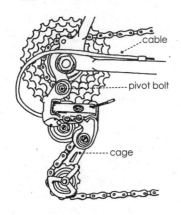
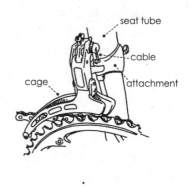

A spring mechanism causes the derailleur to swing backward, to pick up the chain slack as gears are shifted to smaller sprockets, and forward, to compensate for the additional chain needed as gears are shifted to larger sprockets. Therefore, how far the rear derailleur is able to swing back and forth determines the largest and smallest sizes possible for the chainwheels and cogs.

The front derailleur is located above the crankset and is typically attached to the seat tube. Much as with the rear derailleur, the chain runs through a piece of the front derailleur called the cage, which is responsible for physically pushing the chain from one chainwheel to another. Gear shifting on the front end is also accomplished by pulling or relaxing a cable connected to and manipulated by the gear levers.

While all derailleur gearing works on essentially the same principle, index derailleurs are preferable to conventional derailleurs because they offer more precision in shifting. For index shifting, the exact amount of cable pull needed to move the derailleurs (and chain) to each cog or chainwheel is preset, and gear shifters are clicked into each gear. Cables for index shifting are thicker and stronger so that they stay perfectly adjusted.

SUSPENSION

All bicycles need some form of suspension system to protect them and the rider from feeling every bump on the road or trail. Otherwise, bikes would feel like the old boneshakers of the nineteenth century. Good suspension protects the bicycle from the wear and tear of the road, increases traction by keeping the wheels on the ground, and makes the rider more comfortable. Pneumatic tires provide basic suspension, and additional suspension can be built into a bicycle either directly through shock absorbers or indirectly through design.

Some bikes, particularly off-road bikes, have spring-loaded steel coils in the forks that absorb bumps and jumps and work like a car's shock absorbers. Other bikes have shocks built into the rear triangle of the frame, either on the seat stay or seat tube. Less often, bikes can be found with springs or other suspension systems built into the saddle or handlebars, though these create unwanted variables in bike fit. Fork shocks, the most common kind, have become a very popular component on many bikes in recent years.

Most bikes, especially road bikes, don't have shock absorbers. Instead, a milder form of suspension is built into the bike's design. Suspension is increased through a wider wheelbase; larger fork rake; and larger, fatter tires. In addition, the inflation of air in tires can be adjusted for ground conditions. While this kind of suspension is certainly not as effective as a shock absorber, it is certainly adequate for bikes rolling on pavement in most circumstances.

There is one other method of suspension that riders use to ease the shock of surface bumps: movement of their bodies. By standing up as they go over bumps, they are essentially using their legs as suspension.

BRAKES

The three main types of braking systems used in bicycles today are caliper brakes, cantilever brakes, and disc breaks. Caliper and cantilever brakes apply pressure on the rim of the wheel to stop the bike and are considered rim brakes. Disc brakes apply pressure to metal discs attached to one side of the wheel hub.

All three brake types work through a system of levers and cables. Cables connect the brake levers (located on the handlebars) to the brake arms that surround the top of the wheels and are secured to the fork in front or seat stay in back. When the levers are flexed by hand, the cables pull, closing the brake arms around the rims or disc. When the levers are released, the brakes spring back to their original position.

The section of the brakes, called the brake pad, or brake shoe, that comes into contact with the moving surface (rim or disc) is usually made of rubber or composite material to maximize the friction needed to stop. All other parts of the braking system—arms, cable, and levers—must be rigid and precisely positioned to transfer the relatively light force exerted by hands on brake levers to the high power needed in the brakes for effective braking.

CHAPTER 3

Bicycle Types

Almost any bicycle will work for your commuting needs. People travel to work on mountain bikes, road bikes, hybrids, fixed-gears, recumbents, folding bikes, and even fat-tired cruisers. But for most commuters, three bike types seem most popular: mountain bikes, road bikes, or hybrids (often called commuter, city, or comfort bikes).

Enter a bike shop, and you might quickly become overwhelmed. There is a broad range of bike options, designed for all kinds of riding and priced at all levels. Having a basic understanding of bike types will make it easier to determine the bicycle that will work best for your daily commute.

MOUNTAIN BIKES

Today, the mountain bike is the most popular type of bike sold in the United States, and the most common bike used by commuters. Many riders have found all-terrain bikes, ATBs, quite useful on-road as well—some road riders even prefer them to road bikes! This is because mountain bikes tend to be more comfortable than racing bikes. Also, they are better able to handle roads that are not well paved or that have obstructions. Finally, the mountain bike rider's upright position is good for seeing and being seen in traffic. Sure, mountain bikes are neither as fast nor as aerodynamic on the street as road bikes—and they're not as well equipped or as comfortable on long rides as a touring bike—but for many riders, the mountain bike is the best choice for all-around riding.

mountain bike

Mountain bikes are designed to keep the rider in control on rough and uneven terrain such as rocks, dirt, and twigs; they're also made to climb hills and withstand jumps. The best ATBs balance strength with comfort and light weight. Frames have a sturdier geometry, tending to be thicker and more compact than road bikes. Shorter chain stays and a steeper seat angle put the rider's weight over the back wheel for traction and control, while a steeper head angle and large fork rake make for better handling and suspension. Some mountain bikes have actual spring shocks for improved suspension.

ROAD BIKES

Road bikes are known by different names, most of which are not entirely accurate. Noncyclists often call road bikes ten speeds, though today's road bikes may have up to thirty speeds depending on how the chainwheels. Then, of course, there are the old-fashioned roadsters that have only one or three gears.

basic touring bike

Road bikes are also inaccurately labeled as racing bikes because their drop handlebar design resemble bikes used for racing. While it's true that most racing bikes are road bikes, some (such as track bikes) are not meant for the road. And not all road bikes are good for racing. Sports bikes, for instance, look like racing bikes but are not made for competition.

What all road bikes have in common is that they are drop-handlebar derailleur bicycles designed for paved surfaces only. Road bikes also have large wheels and thin tires (how thin depends on the type of road bike), and they tend to be more lightweight than other bicycles (twenty-four pounds or less). Beyond these common characteristics, though, road bikes have a great range of purpose and design. They're good bikes for fast or long-distance commuting, racing, touring, staying in shape, or simply having fun.

HYBRID BIKES

Hybrid bikes (often known as city bikes, commuters, or comfort bikes) that offer a mix of features between mountain bikes and road bikes have become extremely popular in recent years. With less bulky tires and a thinner frame, they are faster and more aerodynamic on roads than mountain bikes. And with a triple chainring, upright handlebars, and sturdy frame, hybrids can also take on mountains. Note, though, that the hybrid is neither as well suited to the road as a road bike, nor as fit for off-road riding as a mountain bike. But for a compromise that offers more versatility, hybrids can't be beat. They are particularly appealing to bike commuters.

Hybrid bikes are essentially modified mountain bikes. As mountain bikes became more popular and people began to use them for street riding, attempts were made to iron out the mountain bike's shortcomings on the road. While the city bike retains the mountain bike's heavy-duty design and upright positioning, other characteristics have been changed to better suit the needs of city riders. For instance, fenders and chainguards are often added to protect the clothes of commuters. And to make riders more upright and visible in traffic, hybrid bike handlebars are raised slightly higher than they would normally be on mountain bikes.

hybrid bike

TOURING BIKES

Designed to carry loads over long distances, touring bikes are often a great choice for commuters who ride longer distance. Touring bikes can often be identified by how they are equipped. They have mounts, or eyelets, used to attach baggage (called panniers), extra water bottles, or other materials needed while touring. Mudguards, or fenders, around the tops of the wheels protect panniers and the rider from the spray of wet, muddy roads. Thicker tires and heavier tubes protect the wheels and provide greater comfort through added suspension. Additional suspension comes from a longer wheelbase—the result of longer chain stays, a sloping fork rake, and a shallow head-tube angle (71–72 degrees).

Without touring equipment such as racks and panniers loaded on, a touring bike can look a lot like a road bike. Drop handlebars are necessary on tourers to allow riders a variety of positions on long rides (upright position is better for visibility in traffic, while the drop position is better for speed—and switching positions once in a while prevents riders from getting stiff over long distances). And a triple chainwheel makes for a wide range of gears, particularly very low gears, that allow easy pedaling on hills even when the bike is weighed down by bags and equipment. In exchange for greater comfort, strength, and pedaling ease, the touring bike has less speed and agility than a racer and usually weighs a bit more.

Specific touring bikes are designed to accommodate the different kinds of touring—from short rides to camping trips to cross-country treks. Basic touring bikes are made for short trips where less equipment and baggage is needed, while long-distance bikes are better able to carry heavy loads in panniers or racks. Riders who plan to do any long-distance touring or bike camping should opt for the latter because even though it will weigh more and be more rigid, a heavy-duty tourer allows the best range of possibilities for touring.

Strictly speaking, any bike can be used to tour. But as any experienced bike tourist will tell you, if you're going to put a bicycle through the rigors of long rides and heavy loads, you'll need a bike designed to accommodate the special needs of long-distance road riding. Good touring bikes are designed to be comfortable, sturdy, and reliable. They should be strong enough to carry loads many times their own weight and efficient enough to handle the hills of country roads.

CRUISER BIKES

For three decades in the mid-twentieth century, Schwinn was synonymous with "bicycle" in the mind of Americans. With comfortable, cushy wide tires—usually with whitewalls—an upright seating position, long swept-back handlebars, maybe a spring front fork, plenty of chrome, and always a sturdy curvy frame, the cruiser is a classic. The cruiser was especially popular in beach communities, and many associate the cruiser with surfing and sunshine, enhancing its cool factor. Today, many bike manufacturers sell cruiser bikes, which are popular among style-conscious bike commuters who travel short distances. Cruisers are heavy, and they are all about comfort and style. The classic cruiser is a single speed, but today many cruisers come with multiple speeds. If your commute is short on flat terrain and you're less interested in speed, a cruiser might be the right commuter bike for you.

FOLDING BIKES

Folding bikes are popular with many commuters who combine transit and bicycling to make their trip; they arrive at the bus stop or train station, fold the bike, and board. Folders are also popular for commuters who lack secure bike parking at their workplace—they simply fold it and store it inside.

The main benefit of a folding bike is its ease of transport. Commuters can simply bring their folded bikes into the office and store them in a closet. Folders are also very convenient on planes, where checking a full-size bike can be expensive, and on public transportation, which may have limits on bike transport. Some are even small enough to fit in suitcases.

Some folding bikes require tools to disassemble, while others use levers and hinges (such as around the seat post, top tube, and handlebars) that make them easier to collapse. Bikes that disassemble are generally stronger but can take up to thirty minutes to take apart, while true folders require as little as one minute to collapse. A few folding bikes do both; they offer riders a choice between folding (which is quicker) and disassembling (which makes the bike more compact).

folding bike

Many folding bikes have small wheels (sometimes only 12" in diameter) for storing, but their wheel size makes them less efficient than regular bikes. Small wheels also provide less suspension and produce more friction, which can cause the rims to overheat. Folding bikes with full-size wheels are available. While these offer better handling and more efficient pedaling, they don't fold as compactly (which may defeat the purpose of getting a folding bike in the first place).

OTHER TYPES OF BICYCLES

There are many other bicycles available to use on your commute. Determine your needs—perhaps one of these bicycle types might be most appropriate for your commuting.

RACING BIKES
Racing bikes are designed, not surprisingly, to maximize speed. That is, after all, how riders win races. Because slight details can make a great difference in a race, good racing bikes feature a precision design. To make the bikes as light and as aerodynamic as possible, frames are made very thin with strong, lightweight materials, such as aluminum, titanium, or carbon fiber.

TRACK BIKES
In many communities, single-speed fixed-gear track bikes or variations thereof have become very popular. Designed for racing on closed oval tracks, track bikes are quick, fast, and

light (there are no components, and often no brakes). They often look like road bikes, and many road bikes can be converted into single-speeds. For fast commuting over flat terrain, this might be a suitable bike for your commute.

RECUMBENT BIKES

For bike commuters who might be uncomfortable riding upright, recumbent bikes may be an option. Recumbent bikes allow riders to pedal while lying back on a backrest (recumbent means "lying down"). While recumbent bicycles, by definition, have two wheels, other recumbents use three wheels for greater balance (but significantly less handling). Recumbents are typically foot powered, though certain designs use hand cranks instead of or in addition to foot pedals.

recumbent bike

TANDEM BIKES

Tandem bikes are easy to distinguish from other bikes because they are made for two riders sitting in line. Though tandems—as well as other multibikes made for multiple riders—have been around since the early days of bicycles, they have received renewed interest since the 1980s and may now be more popular than ever. Why? Because tandems are fun. They're a great way for couples, friends, or a parent and child to work together in a physical activity. And because tandems combine the effort of both pedalers into a single energy out-put, they're especially well suited for duos with different abilities—those partners who may have trouble riding at the same pace on separate bicycles.

tandem bike

BMX BIKES

Many bike commuters are children or youthful adults, bicycling to school or other destinations. For these young commuters, a BMX bike might be an attractive option. BMX, or bicycle moto-cross, began in the 1970s as an adaptation of moto-cross motorcycle racing. Moto-cross bicycles are in many ways the forerunners of mountain bikes, and they remain popular with children. These bikes typically have knobby tires with smaller wheels (20"–24"), straight forks, and a high bottom bracket.

bmx bike

HAND CYCLES

Usually recumbent, hand cycles (which may have two or three wheels) are most often designed for people who have little or no use of their legs. They employ either a hand crank or rowing mechanism, and hand brakes. Some hand cycles make use of both hands and feet; in those cases, the added pedaling power can make them move very fast.

CHILDREN'S BIKES

Traditionally, children's bikes have been very simple, often just one speed with a coaster brake. Children's bikes should be sturdy and safe, with a lightweight, tight frame and strong (preferably cantilever) brakes. One chainring with a wide range of gears is often good enough to start, at least until the child begins to venture out on country roads. Saddles and stems should be adjustable so the bike can grow with the child for a few years. For kids ages 4–6, start off with a 16" wheel; 7–12 year olds can upgrade to a 20" wheel. After that point, go with a small-framed adult bike (26" wheels).

CHAPTER 4

Buying Your Bicycle

Buying a bicycling is exciting and your anticipation will build as you do your research. Review the options, visit shops, make test rides, consult with other bike commuters and bike-shop staff, and read bicycling magazines, bike catalogs, and online resources. You will enjoy your bike more by spending adequate time thinking about your commute, budget, taste, and needs. Bikes are not impulse buys. Don't buy the first beautiful, shiny bicycle you see. Buying a commuting bicycle should be an informed purchase. Try a few. Consider options. Your bicycle commuting experience will be more enjoyable if you find the *right* bike.

DETERMINING YOUR NEEDS

As for any large purchase, the first step in buying a commuting bicycle is to determine exactly how you will use the bike. Will your commute be over flat or hilly terrain? How far will you be commuting? Will your commute involve some use of transit? Do you have a safe place to keep your bike at work? How much stuff (change of clothing, notebook computer, tools, documents, lunch) do you expect to carry? Do not underestimate the importance of getting the right bike for your needs. You're not likely to get excited about riding an uncomfortable bike that can't take you where you want to go. A well-chosen bike, though, will make you want to ride.

Think about what you'd like to do with the bike. Will it be strictly for commuting, or might you want it for exercise and recreation? For long-distance touring? For off-road riding? Would you like to get into racing? If you are shopping for your first bike and don't know exactly what sort of biking activity you'll enjoy most beyond commuting, it's best to get a versatile bike, such as a hybrid or touring bike, that is suited for a number of different kinds of riding.

No matter what kind of bike you get, be prepared to take care of it so that you can enjoy it as long as possible. Properly maintained and protected from weather, a quality bicycle can provide an enjoyable riding experience for many years.

FIX UP THE OLD BIKE OR BUY NEW?

You may already have a bicycle sitting in your garage that would work well for commuting. Perhaps you already bicycle for recreation or exercise. Or maybe you are returning to bicycling after many years of not riding. Older bikes can work very well for commuting.

If you're considering commuting on a bike you already own, take it to a bike shop for an evaluation. Consult with the shop staff and share your commuting goals. Perhaps your present bike can be rehabilitated into a very serviceable commute bike. But if it's older than ten years, you might want to consider buying a new bike. Bicycle technology has made considerable advancements in the past decade, especially with shifting technology, frame materials, puncture-resistant tires, saddle comfort, and other components. Newer bikes simply work better. Your bicycle commuting experience will likely be more fun on a new bike. And certainly, a shiny new bike is a great motivation for bicycle commuting.

BIKE BRANDS

There are hundreds of reputable bicycle manufacturers—large and small—to choose from. Usually, though, a bike's brand name is not as important as the makers of its individual parts. A large percentage of bike frames are made in China and sold to U.S. companies who simply put their name on them. And as large American companies consolidate the industry by buying out smaller bike manufacturers, brand names are becoming confusing and irrelevant. Keep in mind, as well, that large manufacturers produce bikes in a wide variety of quality levels, from mass market toys to highly crafted top-of-the-line machines. The only time brand names count is when you're dealing with high-end specialty companies that make custom frames and parts for their bikes.

The leading bicycle brands in the United States include Trek, Specialized, Giant, Bianchi, Cannondale, Raleigh, Fuji, and Jamis. Many of these brands now offer commuting-specific models, and some companies, such as Breezer, offer only commuting models. Most of these brands also offer women specific sizes, and some companies, such as Terry, are exclusively dedicated to women's bicycles.

More important than buying a particular brand is considering the quality of the bike's components and the quality of the frame. When shopping, compare a few different brands of bikes in the same price range to determine which offers the best value. Look into which manufacturers offer the best warranties. Some bikes have a limited five-year warranty, and other warranties become void if the bike is used for racing. While you should always remain open to a better brand or a better-suited style of bike, try to narrow your choices before you begin to shop seriously for a new bike.

WHERE TO BUY A BIKE

The most common place to buy a bike is a bike shop. There is sure to be one in your town, but before you start visiting around, do a little preliminary research—particularly if you don't know much about bicycles. Though a good bike shop and a helpful salesperson can teach you a lot about bikes, brushing up on some bike basics beforehand will only make you better able to distinguish a sales pitch from legitimate advice. Start by asking the advice of experienced riders or by reviewing some cycling websites and magazines to find product reviews and consumer reports.

When you begin checking out bike shops, pay close attention to what each store offers. Buying from a good shop can make a huge difference in your bike riding experience. Don't just settle for the shop closest to your house; a good bike shop is worth traveling a bit farther to find. Ask friends and other riders to recommend a good shop, and if you can, bring them along with you to help. And don't just go to one shop. Visit as many stores as you can to compare quality, selection, and price; and take the time to find out as much about each store as you can. Spending a little extra time looking for the best bike shop will pay off in the long run if it means you purchase the best possible bike.

Only visit bike shops that have a good reputation with experienced bikers. Many of the best bike shops are small businesses that offer more personal attention, have a friendly atmosphere, and sometimes carry the best brands. Depending on where they are located, some small shops are geared toward a specific customer. Shops in college towns, for instance, cater to the needs of students and may not be the best places to find family bikes. You'll have an easier time finding your bike in a large store that has a wide selection of quality bikes, though you may not get the same customer service. But of course, any bike shop, big or small, that carries the kind of bike you want could be the right bike shop for you. Look for shops that have a decent selection of accessories and a clean, well-stocked repair area.

Good bike shops will offer repair and maintenance service, including a free tune-up and adjustment after thirty days (very important because bikes have a period of breaking in), and regular free checkups at least through the first year. Buying from a small shop can be an advantage. In order to compete with the big stores, many small shops draw buyers by offering great service plans, including free labor for bikes under warranty. By all means, take advantage of these offers. Some shops offer a warranty for parts and service in addition to the warranties provided by the manufacturer. When you buy a bike, shops may also throw in extras such as a water bottle or a new seat or stem. And if they don't make such offers, it never hurts to ask.

A trusted bicycle shop can be a valuable partner for your bicycle commuting experience. Find a shop you like, that makes you feel comfortable, that offers advice on routes, hazards, equipment, and organizations. As indicated earlier, a bicycle can last for many years. A good bike shop understands that it will only sell you the bike once. They should want to get you on the right bike, which would lead you to many frequent return visits to the shop for accessories, equipment, and repairs. A good bike shop should strive to be a resource for your commuting success. Find a trusted and helpful bike shop, and it will truly make your commuting a pleasure.

To find a quality bicycle retailer in your neighborhood, visit the National Bicycle Dealers Association website, at *http://nbda.com*.

MASS-MERCHANT STORES

Anyone in search of a quality bike that will last and provide a smooth, efficient, and enjoyable ride will find most department store bikes severely lacking. Many first-time bike buyers find themselves shopping in a large big box retail store, attracted by the low prices. The most important factor to consider when you buy a bike isn't price, but comfort. Be wary of the "bargain bike." Today's bargain can become tomorrow's aggravation. Buying a quality bike, storing it out of the rain, maintaining it regularly, and replacing parts as needed will all assure that your new bike could easily last for ten or more years. It's far better to get a bicycle that fits well and can offer an enjoyable ride for a decade or more than one that happens to be cheap at the moment. And you can best find the right bike with the assistance of expert staff at a bike shop, not the poorly trained staff at a big box store.

Certainly if you are looking for the cheapest bike you can find—and will be happy with anything that has two wheels and a seat—big box store bikes are, at best, briefly adequate. Shifters and brakes may work adequately for a few rides, but soon begin to fail. Most of these bikes are mass-produced and poorly assembled using cheap metals. They therefore lack the precision, strength, and quality of bikes found in shops. Also, department stores will not offer repair and maintenance service and probably will not even let you have a test ride. Add to that the fact that many bike shops won't repair big box store bikes because they feel it wastes parts and effort (repairs often cost more than the bike!), and the low prices of department stores no longer seem so appealing.

Cost isn't the most important factor when buying a bike. Bikes are inexpensive, period. A great quality bike that will last for many years can be found at a quality bicycle retailer for less than a car payment or two. Avoid the big box bike.

ONLINE AND MAIL ORDER

When you already know exactly what you want, buying a bicycle through an online bicycle retailer or mail-order catalog can be a bargain. Mail-order companies usually charge less than stores because they don't have the overhead costs of salespeople and rent. Buying directly from a manufacturer's catalog or website can be even cheaper because the middle person (in this case, the shop) is eliminated. Catalogs and online stores can also be convenient; there's no need to leave your house.

But unless you are 100 percent certain what you want—and most bike buyers aren't—shopping from websites or catalogs can be like shooting in the dark. A website or catalog offers no sales assistance, no test rides, no fitting, no adjustments, and no repairs or maintenance afterward. Bike shops provide very important services, without which finding the right bike can be nearly impossible. Beginners should make sure they know what they're getting—and what they're getting into—before they buy through mail-order catalogs.

USED BIKES

Like used cars, used bikes are much cheaper than new ones. If you can find a used bike in very good condition, which may not be difficult to do, you may have a real bargain. Good bikes that haven't been misused by their previous owners tend to stand up pretty well. There are two potential disadvantages, though, to buying older bikes: First, they may lack the latest developments and materials; and second, spare parts may be difficult to find if the bike is no longer being produced. You could find yourself needing to replace a whole group of components just to fix one broken part. Fortunately, most bike components are widely interchangeable, so it is unlikely that you would experience much of a problem.

Closely inspect used bikes when shopping. For the most part, you can use the same techniques you use for finding a new bike: look for the right type of bike, take it on a test ride, make sure the bike fits your body, look for a quality frame and components. But also look for signs of wear and tear: rust, bends or dents in the frame or wheels, loose nuts and bolts, frayed cables, worn out chainrings.

WHAT TO LOOK FOR IN A BIKE

When you go to the bike store, make sure you know a little about what you are looking for. Consider the following important components of the bike and your ride—you want to make a smart decision, right?

FRAME

Frames should be made of a material that combines strength with light weight. Though more-rugged frames tend to weigh more, it is certainly possible to find a good balance between the two considerations. Aluminum and chromoly steel frames are the most common choice for good midlevel commuting bikes. Less common materials such as carbon fiber and titanium offer lighter weight but are extremely expensive.

Frames should feel sturdy and have a comfortable frame geometry. A tight frame, with a larger angle between the head tube and the ground, is stiffer and has a short wheelbase. Tight frames handle better but provide less cushion for riders. They perform better through turns, though not as well downhill or at high speeds. A loose frame geometry has a smaller angle between the head tube and the ground—it is shallower with a longer wheelbase. This geometry provides more suspension but less control at normal speeds.

More than any other consideration, the bike frame should fit your body. New bicycle commuters should take test rides on several bikes to determine what frame might work best.

HANDLEBARS

Like the frame, handlebars are most often made of aluminum; some higher-end, lighter-weight handlebars are made of carbon fiber. All handlebars have some form of cushioning for comfort, either rubber or composite grips (mountain, hybrid, commuting bikes), or cork or synthetic handlebar tape (road, touring bikes). On mountain and many hybrid bikes, handlebars are often straight (flat bars) or have some slight rise toward the rider (riser bars), often with bar ends added to provide additional hand positions. Road-bike handlebars are generally curved into drops, offering a range of hand positions. Handlebars come in a range of sizes, and should be approximately the width of your shoulders. Some commuter bikes have moustache-style handlebars, which curve back toward the rider, allowing a more upright seated position. Cruiser bikes have longer, swept back handlebars.

STEM

While stems do not allow a lot of room for adjustment, they are interchangeable. Shops commonly replace uncomfortable stems for free before you buy the bike. It's most important to have a stem with the correct height. Like materials for other bike parts, stem materials vary in strength and weight.

WHEELS AND TIRES

The quality of the wheels and tires you get depends on the price you are willing to pay. Most wheels sold today have aluminum rims, with a large variation in price and quality of different aluminum rims, depending on whether or not the metal has been heat treated. Higher-end wheels may offer details such as a double-wall rim or reinforced eyelets, which add strength and responsiveness. On any wheels, be sure to look for rust-free stainless steel spokes.

The most important considerations on tires will be tread, durability, and ability to resist punctures. Commuter bikes used mostly on pavement will do best with low rolling-resistance smooth tires, or tires with a street-specific tread pattern. Commuters bicycling off-road may consider knobby tread patterns, which offer more traction on dirt paths but more rolling resistance on pavement. Make sure the tires on the bike you buy are equipped with a tread that is appropriate to the kind of roads or trails on which you plan to be riding. If they are not, ask the shop to replace them with tires that have a suitable tread.

SEATS AND SEAT POST

While seats should not be too wide, they need to be wide enough to provide support and comfort. Seats with synthetic leather covers and gel cushioning provide the most comfort, though some riders find them too soft and too heavy. Many seats sold today feature special male-specific or female-specific cutout features to improve comfort and reduce stress on delicate groin tissue.

A seat post made of an aluminum alloy offers a good balance of strength and light weight. Many bicycles feature quick-release levers to secure the seat post, allowing easy adjustments to seat height. Caution: Quick release makes saddles easier to steal.

GEARS AND DERAILLEURS

New bicycles now feature a broad range of gear options, depending on the number of chainwheels on the crankset and the cogs on the cassette. If your commute is mostly on flat terrain, there are bikes that offer a single crankset chainwheel and 8–9 gears on the rear wheelset. Most bicycles have a triple crankset and 8–9 gears on the rear wheelset, offering 24–27 gears for handling a range of terrain. Keep in mind, though, that more gears on a bike may not mean a wider range of speeds. Instead, bikes with more gears tend to offer closer gears with more subtle differences between them. The best way to determine the range of gears is through a test ride. Try out all the gears, most importantly the highest and lowest. Buy a bike with a wide enough range of gears to allow you a comfortable ride wherever you plan to ride. If you live in an area with a lot of hills, look for a bike with lower gears. While all-purpose mountain bikes may be fine, bikes specifically designed to conquer steep mountain trails may be too slow for riding flat roads.

Look for derailleurs that shift smoothly and don't rub against the chain. The leading component manufacturers, such as SRAM and Shimano, offer derailleur models at a range of price and quality levels. Higher-priced components will generally offer slightly better performance, more durability, and have a better cosmetic finish.

BRAKES

Bicycles offer a range of brake options. Cantilever-type brakes (center pull, linear pull) are most common. Disc brakes are common on some commuting bicycles and mountain bikes. And many bikes use caliper brakes. As with derailleurs and other components, higher-priced brakes offer better performance, durability, and finish.

CRANKSET

The standard material used in cranksets is aluminum; higher-priced bicycles might feature a carbon fiber crankset. The crankset should be strong and stiff, to efficiently transfer power from your legs to the rearwheels. Crankarms come in several lengths; longer cranks provide greater leverage for more power. Cranksets feature a single, double, or triple set of chainrings, which come in a range of sizes. Consult with bike-shop staff on the most appropriate crankset for your needs.

PEDALS

The main consideration when it comes to pedals is deciding whether or not you want flat or clipless pedals. Many flat pedals can use toe clips, and straps serve to keep feet on the pedals. While they are certainly not necessary for casual road riding, toe clips become more useful when it comes to longer distance. Be sure the pedals are designed to accept clips, though, before you buy the bike.

Clipless pedals improve pedaling efficiency. They require riders to wear special cleated shoes that attach to the pedal. Essentially, clipless pedals serve the same function as toe clips, but they allow more movement and better performance.

FORKS AND SHOCKS

Most midrange bicycles with nonsuspension forks use aluminum or chromoly. Forks with shock absorbers can add immensely to a rider's comfort, particularly on trails and rough terrain. And with the poor quality of many city streets, shocks can even add comfort to bikes used mainly on the road. In case your shocks end up needing repairs—and they very well may if you ride them hard enough—buy quality shocks made by one of the larger manufacturers so you can be sure to get replacement parts easily.

OTHER DETAILS

If you plan to use your bike for commuting or touring, make sure the frame features mounts for racks and fenders. Most bicycles have mounts for a water bottle, and possibly an air pump. Also look for a bike with a good paint job, although, unfortunately, it's often impossible to determine until the paint actually chips.

Also keep an eye out for other areas where quality can be difficult to determine. Things such as the bottom bracket, hubs, headset, and spokes are where companies can trim their costs by using less than top-of-the-line parts. Here's where shopping with experienced riders can really pay off. Have those with experience closely inspect all the fine points. When looking for a bike, leave no stone (and no gear!) unturned.

FINDING THE RIGHT FIT

Finding the right size bike is crucial to your comfort and bicycle commuting enjoyment. Too small a frame will feel cramped and be difficult to pedal, while too large a frame will stretch you out and be too tall to straddle. Perfect fit—with maximum comfort, control, efficiency, and aerodynamics—is the ultimate goal.

Because most bikes are sized in 2" increments, getting the perfect size can be difficult. Unless you decide to pay a lot more for a custom-made bike, you will probably have to settle for something less than perfect. However, with proper adjustment (or replacement) of the seat, stem, handlebars, and cranks, any bike frame that is within a few inches of the ideal size can be made to suit your body. Have the bike shop make all the fittings and adjustments before you buy the bike. Keep in mind, though, that even after fitting and adjusting the bike in the shop, a truly perfect fit will come only after a long process of fine-tuning. Each person is built differently and may prefer slight variations of standard bike-fitting formulas. As you begin to ride, you will become better able to determine the settings your body feels most comfortable with. Make slight and gradual readjustments as you find your own style of riding.

GETTING THE RIGHT PRICE

After you've determined what kind of bike you want, you're ready to shop more seriously. As you compare features on different bikes of a similar model, also compare prices. What do more-expensive bikes offer? While you generally get what you pay for, a slightly higher price may not mean a better quality bike.

Again, be wary of the "bargain" bike. What you want is the best value, not just the best price. Bicycles are durable. Ask yourself, "Is this the bike I will want to ride two years from now?" Find a bicycle that can "grow" with you as you bicycle, providing the ability to use thinner or fatter tires or add racks for touring or upgrade components for better performance. As you test-ride bikes and compare designs, the subtle differences that make some bikes more expensive than others will become more apparent.

It's possible to get a very good commuting bike for around $500. As prices increase, quality increases more or less proportionately. Once you get up to $1000, though, the differences between more-expensive bikes will only be noticeable to experienced riders (that's even more true of bikes $2000–$3000). Such bikes may be a touch lighter or use more high-tech components, but unless you are a serious rider, they're probably not worth the extra cost. On the other hand, anything significantly below $500 will be less durable and less well crafted. A $250 bike may not even be half as good as a $500 bike.

Midrange bikes costing $350–$600 may have less precision and fewer top-notch components than more expensive bikes, but they can nevertheless be quite solid. These bikes, which are often mass-produced in China, Taiwan, or Mexico, have increased in quality in recent years. For beginners who may find themselves upgrading their bikes as they get more into bicycling, these bikes can be an excellent choice.

There are more than 100 bike companies out there competing for your business. Some offer low-end bikes, some high-end, and others sell bikes in a wide variety of price categories. Most bike companies, except for the specialty manufacturers, make more than one type of bike. And most bicycle companies now offer commuter-specific models.

CHAPTER 5

Getting Equipped to Happily Bike Commute

Having acquired your bicycle, you're ready to bike commute. However, there are many additional items you will eventually want to purchase to enhance your safety and comfort. Most of these items can be found at the same bicycle shop where you may have purchased your bicycle, at sporting-goods retailers, or from a range of online outlets.

SAFETY GEAR

Just as with cars, lighting plays a key role in the safety of cyclists. Lights not only help cyclists see the road in darkness and bad weather, they also help drivers on the road see cyclists. It's a good idea to have a front headlight on your bike at all times, and essential (often mandatory), at night. Even bicyclists who don't plan to ride at night sometimes get caught after sunset or in the rain. Be prepared for all possible situations.

Headlights are usually removable—unless used regularly—and installed onto the front fork or handlebars of the bike. The light should turn with the front wheel to illuminate the path of travel. Direct the beam of light low enough to make small road hazards more visible. The beam of light should be strong and wide enough to illuminate an entire lane of traffic at least twenty-five feet ahead of the bike (far enough ahead to be seen by approaching vehicles around a corner). Bike lights should also be waterproof, in case of rain.

POWER SOURCES

There are three categories of bike-light powering sources to choose from, each with its own advantages and disadvantages. The best type for you will depend on your lighting needs, the distances you usually ride, the illumination you require, and the convenience of use you desire. Here are the possibilities:

Rechargeable battery lights. Batteries, such as nickel-cadmium (NiCd) or nickel-metal hydride battery (NIMH) types, create a strong light and can be recharged again and again. Some NiCd and NIMH batteries conveniently fit in the same lights that take nonrechargeable dry-cell batteries (standard AA or AAA and other sizes). Other NiCD or NIMH batteries are sold with the light, have special connections, and are not interchangeable. Rechargeable batteries are popular among commuter cyclists, who make short, regular trips and can incorporate recharging into their daily routine.

Dry-cell battery lights. Lights that run on disposable batteries are often less bright than more powerful NIMH or NiCD systems but are lightweight and convenient to use. They also are generally inexpensive to buy, and developments with efficient light-emitting diode (LED) technology has led to increased brightness and longer running time. These can be the best choice for cyclists who plan to use lighting only occasionally and value convenience above other considerations.

Generator lights. Dynamo, or generator, lights convert the mechanical energy of a bicycle wheel's movement into the electrical energy needed to illuminate a light. These lights involve a roller device installed onto the front wheel (internally in the hub, or on the side of the tire), attached to the generator, which is connected by wires to the headlight. As the wheels of the bike turn, the resulting energy provides the light. For long trips and frequent use, generator lights are often a favorite among cyclists.

LIGHTING

No matter which type of power system you choose, be sure the bulbs you use are appropriate for the voltage and wattage of the light. LED lights are increasingly popular because they are efficient, bright, and affordable. Halogen bulbs are popular because they last a long time, produce a lot of light, and don't dim with use. Be careful not to touch halogen bulbs with your fingers, though; use a clean cloth to install and remove them.

While reflectors are an adequate form of protection for the backs of bicycles, some cyclists also install rear lighting for additional protection. If you use rear lighting, be sure the light is not blocked or obscured by other equipment. Placing the light under the saddle or behind the rack is best. Strobes, LEDs, or other flashing lights are somewhat effective, although they may not provide a sufficiently wide field of vision and may also make it difficult for drivers to judge your distance.

REFLECTORS

Bike reflectors are required on any bicycle sold in the United States on the front, back, and wheels. Reflectors should be used in addition to headlights and taillights, not instead of them. Reflectors are visible only when light shines on them. A large, flat reflector is a necessity on the back of every bicycle. Attach it to a spot where it won't be blocked by bags or racks, and where it won't become covered by dirt flying off the back wheel (just in case, clean it often). Light-colored reflectors (white) tend to be brighter. Additional reflectors can go on wheels, clothing, or pedals (where circular movement makes them more noticeable), though they are not as important or as effective as rear reflectors. Many tires now have reflective sidewalls, to improve the night visibility of bicyclists. As additional protection at night, some cyclists like to use reflective material on their bikes and clothes.

HORNS AND BELLS

Cyclists should carry or attach to their bike some sort of warning device to alert other vehicles and pedestrians of their approach. Calling out can work in some cases but won't always draw attention on crowded, noisy streets. Loud, jarring horns, such as compressed air horns, work best, while bells are good for riding on sidewalks and in quiet areas. Install noisemakers on handlebars so they can be accessed quickly. Though you should not overuse these warning devices, don't be afraid to let 'em rip when your safety is jeopardized.

PERSONAL COMFORT

People ride bicycles dressed in all sorts of clothing, from dresses or business suits to full racing apparel. Any type of clothing is fine as long as the rider is comfortable and the clothes don't restrict the rider's ability to pedal, turn, and brake effectively. Clothes that are unsuitable can cause rashes, soreness, overheating, and all sorts of other discomforts. For cyclists who find it practical and affordable, special bike clothing is much better for riding than anything else they might find hanging in their closets. For many bicycle commuters who travel less than three miles, riding in their work clothing is fine. Longer-distance bicycle commuters often will wear bicycle clothing, changing at work into appropriate office or work attire.

What makes bike apparel so well suited for cycling? Many things: comfort, durability, performance, safety, aerodynamics.

Everyday clothing tends to be loose; bike clothes, though, are more tight fitting and aerodynamic. Street clothes are heavier than bike clothes, so they weigh you down and may make you hot. And while everyday clothes may not stand out in traffic, the bright, vibrant colors of most bike wear make you more visible and safer on the road.

Though cotton and wool were originally the choice fabrics for cyclists, a wide array of synthetic fibers such as polyester, spandex, polypropylene, Kevlar, CoolMax, and others are used in biking clothes today. These fabrics wick perspiration away from the body without absorbing it. Some, such as Kevlar, are strong and provide protection from road rash, while others are designed more for comfort and easily tear if scraped on the ground. Polyester, nylon, Lycra, or a Lycra/cotton blend are the most commonly used materials, and all are quite effective in hot weather. Materials should be comfortable and strong, suitable to the climate, and capable of protecting riders from the wind and rain. They should also be easy to wash and dry; but be careful because synthetic materials are prone to shrink a lot in a clothes dryer.

While function usually comes before fashion in cycling clothes, there's room for a little style as well. Not surprisingly, most bike-wear designs have their root in racing outfits. While some bike clothes make you stand out in a crowd, others are quite tasteful, fashionable even. Like most clothes, you can choose high-priced designer brands or the more economical clothing lines. The higher price of some clothes is not necessarily indicative of higher quality, so don't feel you need to spend a fortune to be properly outfitted for cycling.

SHORTS

Because so much of your body's movement and energy on a bike comes from the legs, good biking shorts are extremely useful. They tend to be tight (but not constraining) for aerodynamics and flexible for maximum freedom of movement. They should also be soft for comfort. Casual bike shorts with padded linings fit more loosely than racing shorts and are popular with mountain bikers, commuters, and tourists. All shorts should have a waist high enough to cover your lower back and have legs long enough to cover your thighs to protect them from sunburn and chafing. Typically, they have an elastic waist that allows them to stay up without a belt, though some use suspenders (or have an attached bib) to avoid the constraints of tight elastic. Most bike shorts are padded with suede, chamois, synthetic fleece, foam, or gel and have a double layer of fabric in the seat (and sometimes in the hips) for extra comfort.

For practical reasons as a bicycle commuter, you may want bike shorts with pockets to hold keys, identification, or money. Avoid carrying too much when riding, though, or you risk having your possessions strewn across the road. For even more practical reasons, you'll want shorts that can withstand frequent washing and quick drying. They'll need to have strong seams and be made of an appropriate fabric. Leather crotch pads, for instance, can be quite comfortable but won't dry as quickly as synthetics.

Bike shorts are typically worn directly over bare skin without underwear. Try on a number of pairs to make sure the shorts you buy are as comfortable as possible. Buy a few pairs if you plan to ride regularly because they'll probably need to be washed after each use.

SHIRTS

Bike jerseys are made of a thin, cool, silky fabric such as Lycra or polyester, or heavier materials such as Thermax for cooler climates. They fit more tightly around the waist and are longer in back than most shirts. Bike shirts should not be too tight or else they will constrict your movement. Most are short-sleeve with zippered or open pockets sewn in back; long-sleeve jerseys are available for cooler weather and ventilated mesh designs are best for hot days. Many shirts also have a high, zip-up collar to protect the neck.

Some riders stick with comfortable old cotton (or cotton/polyester) T-shirts. These are thin and lightweight but can easily become heavy and clammy if you perspire, and they probably won't fit your body as well as a bike jersey. For most short-distance bike commuting, T-shirts are suitable and convenient for cycling. Some cyclists wear a thin polypropylene T-shirt under their jerseys for extra warmth, moisture wicking, or protection against road rash (avoid cotton in this situation). If they fall, the two layers of clothing will rub against each other and lessen the friction on the body.

When shopping for bike jerseys, look for shirts with a strong construction in the fabric as well as in the zippers and buttons (plastic zippers and buttons are lighter and less irritating than metal ones). There should also be back pockets to use for holding water bottles, wind jackets, snacks, or other objects you may need to reach easily without having to stop the bike.

UNDERWEAR

While certain bike clothes are designed to be worn without underwear, many riders prefer some sort of undergarment for added comfort, protection, warmth, or simply out of habit. Briefs or panties can be worn, though they may irritate the skin if they are cotton and have large seams. For extra support, women can wear a wireless sports bra made of Lycra or a cotton/synthetic blend. Extra layers of underwear, including thermals, are great in cold weather.

SHOES

Shoes can make a huge difference in a cyclist's performance. While almost any shoes will be adequate for biking, it's amazing how much more power and comfort can be attained with specially designed bike shoes. Stiff soles that won't bend are the key to maximizing a bike shoe's impact. They provide a strong and large base of force against the pedals and alleviate pressure on the feet to help prevent the numb, burning sensation often felt on long rides. Thin metal or strong plastic plates stiffen the soles. The upper portion of the shoe, meanwhile, should be comfortable, lightweight, and durable. Leather, synthetic leather, mesh, or a combination works well, though a waterproof or quick-drying synthetic material such as nylon is better in case of rain.

Most bike shoes can be used with flat pedals but have special mounting hardware on the soles for cleat installation for use with clipless pedals. Using clipless pedals improves pedaling efficiency, prevents the feet from sliding off the pedals, and aligns the foot properly on the pedal to avoid knee problems. For riders using toe clips, bike shoes often have a narrow, hard toe design.

Look for shoes that fit snugly so your feet don't slide around inside but allow space so you can wear thick socks in cold weather (bring appropriate socks with you when shoe shopping). Perfect fit is crucial, so try many pairs—even give them a test ride if a bicycle is available—until you find one that's right. Keep in mind that leather stretches and molds to your feet with wear, but synthetics don't. If you want biking shoes that also allow some degree of walking comfort, get shoes with soles that are sufficiently stiff but give a little as well. Laced bindings are common, though many bike shoes use Velcro or other bindings for quicker adjustment and fastening. Bike shoes are available in many sizes and styles. The best place to find bike shoes is at bike shops, though large athletic shoe stores may carry some basic designs.

SOCKS

Socks should be made of wool or a synthetic such as nylon or polyester to provide comfort and wick away perspiration. Racers or other long-distance cyclists prefer white socks, because fabric dyes can irritate or infect blisters. Bike socks can be found in a great range of colors, and many have graphics on the ankle.

HEADWEAR AND EYEWEAR

Because so much body heat escapes through the head, it's most important to keep this area well covered. However, what you wear on your head for warmth must not get in the way of your helmet or make protective gear any less stable. A thin balaclava that covers the entire head, ears, neck, and face (with necessary holes for seeing and breathing) is best. Made of a warm synthetic fabric such as polypropylene, it is inexpensive and small enough to fold into a pocket when not in use. Otherwise, use a hat that fits under your helmet or at least a headband to cover your ears. Good sports glasses keep cold air out of the eyes and can be worn year-round as well. In very cold weather, a facemask may be necessary.

GLOVES
Padded, fingerless bicycle gloves enhance comfort by absorbing handlebar shock and reduce hand abrasions in the event of a fall. As the weather gets colder, it's best to wear gloves that completely cover your hands. Thin polypropylene glove liners add extra warmth in lower temperatures. When it gets below freezing, gloves often aren't warm enough. Instead, wear some form of mitten or three-finger lobster glove that keeps fingers together for warmth. If you're in doubt about which kind of glove is sufficient to keep your hands warm, bring along more than one pair. That way, as your hands warm up and begin to sweat, you can switch to a lighter pair.

JACKETS
One of the great benefits of cycling as a sport and exercise is that the speed of the bicycle creates a natural air conditioning that helps keep the body cool in warm weather. In cold weather, however, a nice breeze blowing across your

body as you ride can be positively chilling. In order to avoid discomfort and stiffness—or worse, hypothermia and frost bite—make sure you are appropriately dressed for riding in cold weather. Don't simply rely on the rise in your body temperature while riding to warm you. It's always best to over-dress—you can remove layers later as you feel necessary.

If you plan to ride throughout the winter, it's a good idea to invest in specially made cold-weather biking clothes. There are jackets made for a range of cold temperatures, which often have vents under your arm pit to ventilate moisture away. The best jackets are made of a breathable fabric, which also helps wick away perspiration. Jackets are also available in a range of rain resistance levels; fabrics such as Gore-Tex provide waterproof protection. Again, evacuating body heat and perspiration through the fabric or vents—slits in the clothing, often with zippers or Velcro closures—is important in cold weather. Damp clothing is not only uncomfortable in colder weather, it can also be dangerous.

PANTS/KNICKERS

In cold weather, the leg muscles and tendons responsible for pedaling are more susceptible to cramps and tendinitis. Long pants and midcalf knickers made out of the same tight-fitting, stretchy material as bike shorts are available. Good leggings keep you warm in cold weather but do not overheat your body during a hard workout. Extra material in the knees is useful to keep your joints warm. In particularly low temperatures, wear tights with a fleece lining. Wool or polypropylene leg warmers, instead of or in addition to tights, will help as well. Leg warmers should have stirrups, stretch up to the thighs, and be snug enough to stay put. There are also a range of wind- and rain-resistant pants, which can help protect your body from cold breezes and chill rains.

LAYERS

Because you want to be neither too cold to ride nor so hot that you sweat profusely, the key is to have many thin layers that can be added or removed as needed. The bottom layer is most crucial. A close-fitting, breathable undershirt, made of a material such as polypropylene, removes perspiration from the body without itself becoming soggy. Outer layers can include a long-sleeve jersey, a turtleneck sweater, a fleece jacket, and a waterproof windbreaker—the most you should ever need to keep you comfortable in cold weather.

Wool is great for warmth but can be itchy, while synthetics work well to insulate and block wind. All clothing should be easy to put on and take off while riding, with conveniently located zippers or Velcro fasteners. If you are going to add and remove layers, make sure you have somewhere to store everything. There's nothing more chilling (and potentially dangerous) than working up a sweat while climbing a hill only to be hit with frigid air as you begin your descent. Whenever possible, bring an extra set of clothes (at least inner layers) in case they become wet with perspiration.

COLD-WEATHER FOOTWEAR

To keep feet warm, wear thick wool or neoprene socks under your shoes and fleece-lined booties or shoe covers over them. Booties should be made of lightweight synthetic material (such as nylon, Gore-Tex, or neoprene—some have a fleece lining as well) that can withstand water and block wind and should fit snugly up to the ankle.

HYDRATION

The easiest way to stay hydrated is with water bottles—they are inexpensive, easy to find, and easy to use—and they're one of the most important pieces of equipment you will carry. If you use a bike for short trips, a water bottle may not be crucial, though it certainly can't hurt. If not used for drinking, the water in a water bottle can be used to wash hands and bikes after a repair or to ward off dogs. If not used for storing water, containers can be used for holding food, pills, even a spare battery for your light. For long commutes, don't start riding without a bottle filled with cold water. Water bottles should be cleaned with hot water and an antibacterial detergent.

HYDRATION SYSTEMS

Many longer-distance or performance bicyclists use a hydration system—such as the CamelBak. This features a large-capacity reservoir of water carried in a backpack or waist pack, with a small hose attached over the shoulder toward the mouth. Cyclists can drink whenever they want by sucking on the soft plastic valve to pull water from the reservoir. Hydration-system reservoirs need to be cleaned regularly, with an antibacterial detergent and a special brush.

CARRYING CAPACITY

Many bike commuters install rear or front racks on their bikes, which are helpful for carrying necessities such as office supplies, a change of clothing, or groceries on the trip home. Racks are made by many companies and come with different load-bearing capacities, from light commuting to heavy-duty touring. Most racks are made from aluminum tubing; some are made from chromoly steel. Most rear racks feature two or three vertical tubes, which join at the bottom of the rack to attach with bolts to rear braze-on mounts. The top of the rear rack attaches to mounts located on the rear seat stays. Front racks can be mounted to the mounts on the fork. The rack creates a top platform area, either open or as a single flat metal sheet, where panniers or other objects can be secured. Elastic straps with hooks are available to secure items, either with bags or without. While most lightly loaded bike commuters carry their stuff on rear racks, heavier loads should be more evenly distributed over both wheels.

PANNIERS

Panniers are specially designed bike bags that attach with hooks and straps to a rack. There are panniers designed for both the front and rear rack mounting. Panniers are available in a range of sizes, for a diverse range of cycling needs from commuting to touring. Most are made of synthetic fabrics, such as nylon, and feature zippered or latched closures. Many panniers have a single large pocket, others feature several pockets attached to the sides and front. Most pannier fabric offers some protection from rain, and waterproof models are available. Many bicycle commuters also acquire waterproof covers for their panniers. Whether front or rear, panniers should be mounted reasonably low—with the heaviest supplies packed lowest—to keep your weight stable. They should also be easy to carry separately once you park your bike; many come with shoulder straps.

GARMENT BAGS

If your work requires that you wear a skirt, dress, suit, jacket, or slacks, you will likely bicycle commute in shorts and change at work. How will you get your office clothing to work? Many bike commuters use a bicycling-specific garment bag such as those sold by Two Wheel Gear, Jandd, Lone Peak, or Performance Bicycles. Many bike commuters can carry their dress clothes in standard panniers, minimizing wrinkling by rolling their garments. Some bike commuters keep an iron in their office for quick touch up smoothing. And some bicycle commuters simply leave their dress clothes at the office and use a nearby dry cleaner as necessary.

BASKETS

Many bicycle commuters prefer the convenience of baskets permanently mounted on their bikes. Baskets can be on the front fork and handlebars, or on the rear braze-on mounts. Most baskets are made with aluminum. Many companies now also sell folding fabric baskets, which attach to a rack and can be removed easily. Most feature stiff plastic for support and can carry a typical grocery bag load.

SHOULDER BAGS

Many bicycle commuters prefer to keep their bikes light and carry things on their backs. Some use standard backpacks, and some companies offer bicycling-specific backpacks. Many more bike commuters use messenger bags—such as those made by Timbuk2 or Chrome—which feature a large pouch with a flap that secures with latches or Velcro. Messenger bags differ from backpacks in that they have only one large shoulder strap, which makes them easy to rotate to the front of your body for access.

TRAILERS

There are a number of bicycle trailers available for those bike commuters who need to carry heavier objects to work, want to bring their dog to the office, or perhaps must deliver a child to school or day care. Many attach behind the bike through an arm connected to a seat or chain stay. Some models, such as Cycletote, attach to a hitch mounted on the seatpost. Bicycle trailers come in a range of sizes and styles and can carry up to 300 pounds.

KICKSTANDS

In countries with high levels of bicycle use for practical transportation—such as Holland, Denmark, Germany, China, and Japan—every bike has a kickstand. For many years, kickstands were standard equipment on bicycles sold in the United States. But with the explosion of mountain biking in the 1980s and the success of bike racer Lance Armstrong in the 1990s, bike manufacturers stopped offering kickstands on bikes. Consumers wanted light, fast, high-performance recreation machines, the thinking went, and kickstands disappeared. Only nerds wanted kickstands, said the athletic cyclists, as they tried leaning their bikes against walls only to watch them roll and fall. Light and fast was the mantra of bicycling at the end of the twentieth century. Kickstands disappeared.

Having exhausted the relentless pursuit of the performance athlete—while largely neglecting bicycle commuters—bike manufacturers are now waking up to the profit potential of the commuting bike market. Only a small percentage of Americans are active competitive athletes—but nearly every American commutes to a job. And kickstands are back. They aren't nerdy, they're smart.

There are many kinds of kickstands, but the two primary types attach to the bike either on the chainstays near the bottom bracket or to the rear triangle where the seat and chainstays meet on the nondrive side. Kickstands are an essential amenity for bicycle commuters. If your bike doesn't have one, get one.

AIR PUMPS AND OTHER ACCESSORIES

On long trips, a good air pump can make the difference between being slightly inconvenienced and being helplessly stranded. While floor pumps are easy to use at home, they're difficult to take with you. For bike trips, buy a lightweight and slender pump that will clamp onto the bike's down tube or seat tube (or sometimes the top tube) for easy access and storing. The pump should fit your tire valves (presta or Scrader) and preferably will come with a built-in tire gauge (if not, get a separate gauge to measure tire pressure).

BIKE LOCKS

A strong bike lock is necessary whenever you plan to leave your bike unguarded. Though there's no such thing as a completely unbreakable lock, some locks are clearly better than others, and the best locks can provide a reasonable surety that your bike will not be stolen.

The best lock to use on a bike is the common U-lock. U-locks are lightweight and small, yet rigid and extremely strong. Clamps can be installed on your bike frame to store the lock while you ride. Use a U-lock to secure your bike to an immovable object. The best ones are bike racks, parking-meter poles, street signs (they are too tall for a bike to be lifted over them), fences, or metal gates. Loop the U-lock through the front wheel and the frame (particularly if the front wheel is easily removable), as well as to the secure object. If possible, loop the lock through both wheels. Remember to take all removable accessories with you when you leave the bike.

TOOLS AND REPAIR EQUIPMENT

Though bicyclists cannot expect to carry all the bike repair tools and equipment they may need with them on the road, some are easy to bring along and can prove helpful in trouble situations. Most bike shops sell bicycling-specific multitools, which work like a Swiss army knife and feature most of the tools needed for roadside repairs. Buy good tools and equipment—even if they cost a little more—and know how to use them before you find yourself in an emergency. If you prefer not to use a multitool, carry as many of the following as will fit in a removable tool pouch or saddlebag:

TOOLS
- Tire levers
- Allen keys
- Convertible screwdriver (Philips, flat)
- Adjustable wrench
- Small pliers

EQUIPMENT
- Tire patch kit, including patches, glue, and sandpaper
- Spare tube
- Spare batteries for lights
- Optional parts: cable, spokes, chain links
- Rags, latex gloves (easy cleanup)
- ID, spare key, change

FENDERS
Riding in rain doesn't have to be miserable—provided you have fenders. The water that falls down as precipitation is easy to cope with. It's the sloppy, dirty muck that splashes up that is most unpleasant. Bicyclists riding in the rain without fenders have dark streaks of splashed road muck up their

backsides. Not attractive. Easy way to ruin a work outfit. Get fenders. They are affordable and come in a variety of styles. Some are made to quickly snap on and off, attaching to the fork or seat post. Others are made to attach with bolts to braze-ons on the frame and fork and can be left on the bicycle indefinitely. Fenders come in a range of sizes; make sure your fenders fit your wheel size and have adequate clearance for your tires.

COMPUTERS

The simplest bicycle computer is basically a battery-operated electronic speedometer or odometer. Basic bicycle computers are very inexpensive, often measuring speed, trip miles, total miles, and average speed. Other computers do a lot more, including acting as a stopwatch, regulating your workout routine, and measuring heart rate. Cycle computers generally attach to the handlebars and have a magnet on a wheel spoke and a sensor on the fork for collecting data. Some computers connect the sensor with the computer with a wire, while more advanced models are wireless.

Closely follow all directions for how to install and calibrate your computer. After you install it, it's a good idea to secure any loose wires to the back of the fork and along the front brake cable with plastic zip ties so they don't get caught on anything as you ride. A cycle computer can be a great motivating tool for bike commuters: "Hey, I bicycled ten miles to work this morning."

CHAPTER 6

The Engine: Your Body

Commuting by bicycle offers a double benefit: You can travel to work while improving your health. For those of us who think of exercise as a necessary evil in our lives, it's amazing to find an activity that's great for the body and actually fun as well. One reason it's so easy to gain health benefits from cycling is that riding is a pleasure; there's none of that dread and boredom many people face when spending hours in the gym bobbing up and down on a stair climber or endless repetitions on a treadmill.

Like other activities that raise your heart rate and increase your body's oxygen consumption (such as running and calisthenics), bicycling can be an aerobic exercise at higher-intensity effort. Aerobic exercise serves a number of functions. It strengthens your heart and circulatory system, which pumps oxygen and other nutrients in your blood through your body. It helps you burn calories, causing you to lose weight. And when done regularly, aerobic exercise increases your energy level and lowers your blood pressure; it also makes you less tired during the day and allows you to sleep better at night. Because repeated exercise lowers your risk of heart disease, heart attack, stroke, even cancer—and keeps your body in top working order—aerobic activity such as bicycling, in effect, can extend your life.

ALL-AROUND HEALTH

While any sort of aerobic exercise is good for you, cycling is particularly well suited for all-around health. When riding the right size bike with correct form, pedaling is smooth and rhythmic and is actually less stressful on the legs than running—which can damage the joints and tendons of knees, legs, and feet. You're also less likely to pull or twist a muscle on a bike than you would in a sport that requires jumping, quick turning, or sudden stopping, such as basketball or tennis. With the exception of swimming, bicycling is the exercise that puts the least amount of stress on the joints of the body.

Biking provides a better cardiovascular workout than many other exercises and sports. It's great for burning fat (that's why stationary bikes are so popular in health clubs) and helps speed up your metabolism to make the most of the food you eat. Also, cycling keeps muscles toned and bones strong—not just in the legs, where most of the work happens, but in the arms, back, shoulders, and buttocks as well. A well-balanced muscular development will make you healthier, stronger, and probably better looking!

FLEXIBILITY AND ADAPTABILITY

Bicycling is adaptable to any level of fitness. If you don't think you can handle a rigorous pace, simply go at a slower pace until your fitness improves. You might be intimidated pedaling up hills, but change to a lower gear and climb at a comfortable rate. As you steadily increase your fitness level, you can adapt your riding routine to keep challenged.

Cycling for fitness doesn't take long, either. With as little as a half-hour a day—a typical commuting experience—you can get in shape reasonably quick. And if the level at which you ride and your style of riding is safe, you're never too old for bicycling. Where many activities can become harmful or risky for older people, bicycling is always practicable. In fact, because of cycling's health benefits, the more you ride the more able you'll be to continue riding as you get older. With a doctor's approval, it's not unimaginable that cyclists can keep going well into their seventies and eighties. From a medical standpoint, the more you ride the younger you get.

As an exercise, cycling is good for all parts of your body, from the bottoms of your feet all the way up to your head. Just as a good workout strengthens muscle and improves the flow of blood and oxygen, it also stimulates the most complex organ of them all, the brain. The increase of blood and oxygen to the brain helps keep the mind well nourished. The mind benefits from biking in many other ways as well.

A NATURAL DRUG

Bicycling, like other vigorous exercise, causes your brain to release endorphins, a natural protein produced by your body that acts as a painkiller and relaxer. Endorphins released during cycling create a feeling of well-being that is commonly referred to as a "natural high." You feel lifted up, less depressed, and less stressed.

BOOSTED SELF-ESTEEM

An enjoyable bicycle commute and meeting the challenges you set for yourself give you a sense of achievement and confidence that can spread into all areas of your life. Because you feel more in control of your body, you'll feel more in control of your life, and more in tune with the world around you. With boosted self-esteem, you'll feel able to take on anything that might come your way.

AN ESCAPE

Bicycling provides a much-needed escape from the daily grind. Many bicycle commuters actually take the long way home, looking for quiet scenic routes, adding miles to their commute to spend more time on their bike. Instead of sitting in a car interior, breathing the exhaust from the vehicles ahead of you, bike commuting gives you a great opportunity to be outside and appreciate your community and landscape.

A STRESS REDUCER

When entered into with the right attitude, regular commuting by bicycle can be effective in reducing stress. The key is not to let the biking itself become stressful. Don't be too obsessed with regimen—don't pressure yourself to ride a certain amount every day, especially on a day when you feel you can't handle the schedule. Look for quieter, more scenic streets, which often run parallel to the more traffic-congested route.

ENHANCED SEXUAL ENJOYMENT

Bicycling improves sexual enjoyment for both women and men by improving stamina, blood flow, metabolism, breathing efficiency, and muscle strength. And losing weight and improving fitness may improve your self-esteem and also your appearance.

WEIGHT CONTROL

If you're looking to lose weight, there are few activities more suitable than bicycling. Biking—particularly sustained rides that challenge your body—burns a tremendous number of calories, which, when combined with a healthy diet, leads to weight loss. Because cyclists can adjust riding to match their physical capabilities, a rider at any level can take advantage of biking's health benefits.

However, don't expect miracles. As for any exercise, weight loss will only come through bicycle commuting if you stick with it and properly challenge your body. Don't be discouraged if you don't shed any pounds after your first few days. If you develop new muscles, you may actually gain weight in the beginning. But if you keep up your bike commuting, over the course of a few months, you will see effective weight loss.

CALORIES BURNED WHILE CYCLING

Indirectly, calories are a measure of the amount of energy foods provide. While the body needs about 2,500 calories per day to operate efficiently (about 1,500 for inactive people and up to 4,500 for training athletes), taking in more calories than the body needs will lead to an increase in fat stored in the body. Every 3,500 or so excess calories can translate to an extra pound in body weight. To lose weight, people need to eat less, burn more calories, or better yet—do both.

The following table gives the approximate number of calories burned per hour by a cyclist of a specified weight riding at a specified average speed. Because many variables come into play—the weight and efficiency of the bicycle; the slope and surface quality of the ground; heat and wind resistance; the form, fitness, and metabolism of the rider—it's impossible to precisely measure calories burned while riding. There may be a variation in the calories burned by two riders of equal weight going at the same speed if other factors come into play. These numbers are given merely as a general guide.

Calories per hour burned based on weight (lbs.) and cycling speed

WEIGHT	8 MPH	10 MPH	12 MPH	14 MPH	16 MPH	18 MPH	20 MPH	25 MPH
100	175	215	255	305	370	445	535	845
120	215	255	305	370	445	535	640	1015
140	250	300	360	430	515	620	750	1185
160	285	340	410	490	590	710	855	1355
180	320	385	460	555	665	800	960	1525
200	355	425	510	615	740	890	1070	1695
220	390	470	560	675	810	975	1175	1865
240	425	510	615	740	885	1065	1285	2030

METABOLISM

Some new riders who hope biking will help them lose weight also worry that increased physical activity will improve their appetite so much that they'll gain back all the calories they lose biking. While it's true that people who are in shape and who exercise regularly can eat more than sedentary people, there are reasons why eating more doesn't lead to weight gain for physically fit cyclists. As people burn more calories cycling, their bodies require more energy and nutrients to keep them operating at the same level. Cycling leads to an increased metabolism—their body digests food and uses nutrients quicker, plus it burns calories more efficiently. While fit people may eat more, they also tend to crave healthy foods to satisfy their bodies' need for important vitamins and nutrients. These factors more than compensate for the increased appetite caused by exercise, thus ensuring that active people continue to burn calories and lose weight. Because it is an aerobic exercise, cycling increases the amount of oxygen riders inhale and stimulates the heart, in turn, improving both the cardiovascular system (which controls the flow of blood through your body) and the respiratory system (which handles the intake, exhalation, and use of oxygen in the body).

HEART HEALTH

Cycling benefits the cardiovascular system in a few ways. First, it conditions the heart muscles to pump a larger volume of blood more efficiently. For instance, an extremely fit person may only need half the number of heart beats per minute that an unfit person needs to pump the same amount of blood through the body. Some cyclists' hearts are so efficient that they have what seems to be abnormally low heart rates.

Also, a more efficient heart ensures that nutrients more rapidly reach all parts of the body and that the maximum amount of energy is reserved for other important body functions. In addition, exercise breaks down the fatty tissue found in artery walls to increase circulation and lower blood pressure. Because very active cyclists have incredibly healthy hearts, they are able to sustain very high heart rates when at work as well as very low rates when at rest.

LUNG HEALTH

Like other muscles that benefit from exercise, the lungs expand and strengthen as a result of the greater demands put on them. As you naturally begin to breathe heavily during a bicycle commute, your lungs become more accustomed to a greater intake of air and a larger expulsion of carbon dioxide. Soon your lungs take in more air all the time, whether or not you are exercising. More air intake means more oxygen is absorbed into the body, which leads to better health. Serious cyclists tend to have magnificent lung capacity, with an ability to inhale in one breath up to 25 percent more air than the average person. But even a daily bike commute at a moderate pace will yield improved breathing.

AEROBIC CONDITIONING

There's a very clearly defined method for determining when you are getting an aerobic workout. It applies to all forms of aerobic exercise, including but not limited to bicycling. If you've ever done aerobics or put time in on a Stairmaster or rowing machine, you're probably already familiar with it. The idea is to figure out your maximum heart rate—the number of beats per minute that it is unsafe to exceed—and then exercise at a level 70–80 percent of maximum for at least twenty minutes each time you workout. This target range represents the point at which the benefits of aerobic exercise are maximized while the dangers of overstressing your heart are minimized. Exercising below the target area means you're not getting the most out of your workout; exercising above the target area means you may be hurting your body.

For aerobic exercise to be truly effective, it must be done regularly. Even if you exercise only for the minimum of twenty minutes a day, you should do so at least 3–4 times a week (missing an occasional day here and there won't hurt you, though). You may not be able to reach your target heart rate and sustain it for twenty minutes at first. That's okay; if you push yourself too hard, exercise becomes unhealthy. If necessary, give yourself a few weeks to work up to your target area.

BREATHING TECHNIQUES

Whenever possible, try to breathe through your nose while riding. Nose hairs filter and warm the air better than the mouth can. However, when a lot of air is needed for rigorous exercise, it's often necessary to take in air through your mouth. Whether breathing through your nose or mouth, be sure to inhale as much as you can and exhale fully with each breath.

The natural tendency for beginning cyclists during a ride is to huff and puff, to gasp for air with short quick breaths. A more efficient method, though, is deep breathing. Large inhalations lasting a few seconds each are easier on the muscles your body uses to breath (and are less likely to cause cramps) and get more oxygen into your system. This type of breathing may seem unnatural and difficult at first, but with practice it becomes automatic.

MUSCLE DEVELOPMENT

Everyone likes to have a little muscle—it's certainly a lot more attractive than the alternative—fat. But there are better reasons for developing muscle than appearance. Muscle makes your body stronger in a number of different ways. You become stronger in the sense that your arms can lift more weight and your legs can jump higher or kick harder. But you also become stronger on the inside; strong muscle tissue is less likely to be injured and recovers quicker when damaged. Also, strong muscles protect other parts of the body from harm. The more you exercise your leg muscles, for instance, the more protection they'll provide the bones, joints, and cartilage in the legs.

Because it takes energy to pedal a bicycle, muscles burn many calories during cycling. Because most of the work is done in the legs, hips, thighs, and buttocks, these areas have the most to gain from bicycle commuting. However, there are literally dozens of muscles that are used in cycling, from neck and shoulder muscles to chest and arm muscles, all the way down to muscles in the feet.

HEALTH RISKS AND INJURIES

Bicycling is a relatively safe activity, especially compared to higher-risk activities such as skiing, hunting, or driving. However, bicycling is not without risks, which can be avoided or mitigated with careful, thoughtful riding.

KNOW YOUR LIMITS

One kind of health risk is posed by riders who don't know their limits. As with any physical activity, a bicycle workout can turn hazardous if the participant overdoes it. While the body has ways of announcing when it's being pushed too far—pain and exhaustion, for instance—enthusiasts who foolishly subscribe to an exercise-as-punishment ethic sometimes ignore the messages their body is sending. All cyclists, particularly beginners, should consider health problems they may have before they get into biking. For instance, a man who knows he has a weak heart shouldn't attempt rigorous bike commuting (though, with a doctor's recommendation, the right kind of cycling regimen may be just what he needs).

SEE A DOCTOR

Anyone who has some existing health issues and wants to start bicycle commuting should see a doctor before beginning. In particular, people who smoke, drink, are overweight, are largely inactive, are pregnant, or have had prior health problems need to determine what level of stress their bodies can take. A medical checkup is an important first step in bringing your body back to health. Besides determining your fitness level, a doctor may be helpful in designing a bicycling regimen that is appropriate to your abilities.

DON'T LET THE RISKS STOP YOU

As in any sport or activity, bicycling can occasionally cause discomfort or injuries. These typically involve back, neck, or knee problems, or an irritation from the seat or handlebars. If addressed properly, these problems are rarely a cause for concern. However, if they go untreated or persist despite treatment, they can become more serious. We'll deal with specific biking ailments later in this chapter.

Still, despite any health risks cyclists may face, it remains certain that almost anyone—no matter what age or condition physically—will be infinitely better off bicycling (or doing some other exercise) than not bicycling. While it's important to consider and address the dangers, they're minor when compared to the benefits.

For the most part, women have just as many opportunities as men to enjoy all that cycling offers. Women, of course, receive the same health benefits as men. Most cycling problems come up only if a woman trains too intensively or rides on a bicycle not well suited to her body or her riding practices.

STRETCHING

For bicycle commuting or any other bicycling, a 10–15 minute stretch beforehand is highly recommended. Stretching prevents injuries such as muscle tears and overextensions by loosening muscles and increasing flexibility. It also helps your body prepare for a workout by getting an increased amount of blood flowing to your muscles in advance of when you'll actually need it. A second period of stretching should come after your ride to reinforce flexibility and help prevent muscles from tightening up and becoming sore.

Stretches that prepare you for a bike ride concentrate on the neck, upper and lower back, hips, upper legs (quadriceps and hamstrings), and lower legs (calves and ankles). Perform all stretches slowly and smoothly, without bouncy or jerky motions. Stretch to a point where the muscle begins to hurt and hold each stretch until your muscle becomes accustomed to the extension. Breathe deeply and evenly as you begin a stretch, then exhale as you release.

FUEL YOUR COMMUTE: NUTRITION

Diet goes hand in hand with any kind of physical activity, including bicycle commuting. Without proper nutrients, cyclists will not perform as well as possible. And without physical activity, nutrients are not well utilized. What makes up a good diet for cyclists is essentially the same as what's good for anyone, though an active cyclist may need more of certain nutrients than the average person.

Building a proper diet is a matter of figuring out what the body needs and supplying the right amount of it. There's no magical guide to perfect food intake—each person has different needs. In fact, because there are so many levels of cycling performance, the variation in bikers' diets is especially great. However, there are a number of dietary needs that each person must satisfy. And there are many suggestions that will help each individual define a suitable diet.

WHAT YOUR BODY NEEDS

Our bodies get three things from the food and drink we take in: energy, water, and nutrients. Energy, in the form of calories, we've already discussed earlier in this chapter. Water and nutrients relate to energy in that they enable the body to function: to build cells, to perform physical actions and processes, and to replace needed materials.

Water

When you consider that a person's body is made up of more than 90 percent water, it's not hard to imagine what can happen to us when we are not properly hydrated. Just a minor deficiency can result in heat exhaustion or heat stroke. Though it provides no nutrients or energy, water is the single most important component in our diet—particularly crucial for physically active people. It not only keeps the body cool through perspiration, it also cleanses the body, enables metabolism, and ensures that the body stays chemically balanced. Without water, your body could not process nutrients into energy. For heavy exercise, in which the muscles build up lactic acid, water helps flush out the acid that can cause sore muscles.

Other liquids, including juices and special sports drinks, provide minerals lost through perspiration and replenish glycogen levels. Most are somewhat helpful for cyclists, but they can be unnecessarily high in calories. While they may improve performance in serious training, they may not be needed for regular fitness workouts. Drinks with caffeine, such as coffee, tea, or colas, will give you a lift; however, drink caffeinated beverages in moderation, because they have some diuretic effect, causing you to lose fluids through urination. For pure hydration purposes, you can't go wrong with water. Water is calorie free, so you can drink as much as you want.

Drinking too much water before a ride can lead to stomach cramps, but a moderate amount about a half hour before your bicycle commute helps prepare your body. If you go on a long or particularly strenuous ride, bring along a bottle (or two) of cool water and drink regularly—at least every fifteen minutes. Don't wait until your body feels weak and dehydration sets in—by then it is too late. Drink slowly; gulping down large amounts only causes stomach problems. And make sure you drink plenty of water after a ride to replenish any liquid you've lost through perspiration.

Carbohydrates

Carbohydrates are the body's main source of energy. Because they are absorbed into the body faster than proteins or fats, carbohydrates are a great source of nutrition for active people. To keep the energy supply at a level suitable for physically active people, a diet should consist of about 65 percent carbohydrates. Without enough carbohydrate intake, blood sugar drops, causing muscles to tire and fail; in extreme cases, low blood sugar can cause dizziness, nausea, even collapse.

There are two types of carbohydrates (carbs): simple and complex. Simple carbs (monosaccharides and disaccharides) are sugars such as glucose, lactose (milk sugar), and sucrose (found in table sugar and honey). They are absorbed directly and are therefore good for quick and easy energy in training or as a snack during long rides. However, they are burned quickly and don't provide long-term energy. And unless you use the energy provided by simple carbohydrates for exercise, too much can make you fat.

Complex carbs (polysaccharides), including starches and pectins, are made up of chains of glucose. They are found in foods such as pasta, potatoes, bread, cereal, fruits, and vegetables, though in smaller concentrations than in simple sugars. Because these take longer to break down, they provide long-term energy and are better suited for regular daily meals between workouts. And because the foods that have complex carbs also contain other nutrients, they help provide a more balanced diet.

Four servings of fruits and vegetables and three servings of breads and cereals per day provide enough carbohydrates for most people. The more energy cyclists need, though, the more carbohydrates they should consume. While a steady diet is most beneficial, racers often load up on carbohydrates a few days before a race to maximize their energy. If you increase the amount of carbohydrates you eat, be careful not to overeat. Overeating can cause a loss of blood to the muscles (because more blood is needed in digestion) and, of course, an unhealthy gain in body fat.

Protein

While proteins are a necessary part of every person's diet, cyclists do not need much more of them than anyone else. Protein in food helps the body form muscles, bones, skin, red blood cells, and the many biochemical proteins (enzymes, hormones) that make up our body. However, they are not a particularly good source of energy.

Proteins are commonly found in foods such as meat, poultry, fish, eggs, cheese, and other milk products. For people who don't eat meat, a mixture of foods like rice, beans, tofu (and other soybean derivatives), whole wheat, and nuts can fill the body's protein requirements. Only 10–15 percent of our diet should be made up of proteins, so it's best to limit high-protein food intake to two servings a day.

Getting enough protein is not usually something we need to worry about, for two reasons. First, the body doesn't need a large amount, and second, Americans tend to eat much more protein than necessary. However, because the body cannot store excess protein, a constant (though moderate) supply is necessary. Excess protein is either discarded or converted into glucose (for energy) and fat. And because high-protein foods also tend to be high in fat, getting too much protein also means you're getting too much fat.

Fat

Unlike proteins, fats are a good source of energy because they are dense in calories (higher in calories even than carbohydrates). Fats, though, are not as easily retrieved for energy as carbohydrates, so they are used as a secondary source of energy after the glycogen from carbs has been depleted.

Of the two types of fats—saturated and unsaturated—unsaturated fats are healthier. These are found in grains, corn, soybean, nuts, and some oils (such as olive, sunflower, and corn). Saturated fats come from meats, poultry, fish, dairy products, egg yolks, and some vegetable oils. Because they are high in cholesterol, eating too much of them can lead to heart disease. However, fats are a necessary part of the diet—they supply fat-soluble vitamins (A, D, E, and K), though not many other nutrients. They should make up about 15–20 percent of your total caloric intake, with three-fourths of it from unsaturated fats. Like proteins, though, most people eat plenty of fat. It's usually not a matter of trying to get enough fat, but rather trying to limit it. Most Americans are lucky if their fat intake totals less than 30 percent of their daily intake.

Some amount of body fat is healthy; it helps insulate the body from cold and protect it from viruses. Plus, it's the fat in foods that tends to taste good. Too much fat, though, limits the amount of blood that reaches the muscles, sometimes leads to heart disease, and, of course, makes you fat.

Because fats can take a long time to digest, any fat intake should come long before—at least three hours prior to—your workout. Otherwise, it takes energy away from your muscles and could hurt your stomach. The good news for cyclists is that, because they burn so many calories, they can take in a little more fat without gaining weight.

Vitamins and Minerals

Vitamins and minerals found in all foods are necessary in the diet. While they are not nutrients, they enable the body to break down nutrients. A well-balanced diet generally supplies all of your vitamin and mineral needs. However, a good way to make sure you get everything you need is to read the chart of recommended daily values on the side of food packages.

Our bodies use vitamins to control enzymes during metabolism and to form bones and muscle. Water-soluble vitamins—B-complex, bioflavinoids, and C—are not stored in the body, so they must be ingested daily. B-complex vitamins, used to convert carbs, proteins, and fats into energy (therefore very important to cyclists), are found in meat, fish, vegetables, milk products, and eggs. Vitamin C—which fights sickness and builds tissue, among other things—can be found in citrus fruits and green vegetables. Bioflavinoids, which assist vitamin C, are found in fruits.

Fat-soluble vitamins (A, D, E, and K) are stored in body fat and can be dangerous if held in large amounts. Vitamin A, which helps grow body tissue, is found in vegetables and meats. Vitamin D, found in dairy products, fish, egg yolks,

THE BIKE TO WORK GUIDE

and green vegetables, strengthens bones and teeth. Vitamin E, which helps cells remain strong, is in wheat germ, nuts, grains, and some vegetables. Vitamin K helps bones develop and clots blood; it is developed naturally in the body but is also found in dairy products and egg yolks.

Minerals also play an important part in metabolism. They activate chemical reactions in the body that enable the breakdown of nutrients and regulate muscle contractions. In addition, minerals are used in forming bone and muscle. The major minerals found in the body include calcium, iron, magnesium, phosphorus, potassium, and sodium (the most abundant). Small amounts of minerals such as aluminum, boron, copper, fluorine, iodine, manganese, nickel, and zinc can be found in the body as well.

Calcium, which forms bones and teeth, can be found in vegetables and milk products. Iron, which helps form hemoglobin (which carries oxygen in blood), is in meats, eggs, and many vegetables. Nuts, spinach, soy, and wheat germ are good sources of magnesium, which plays a role in many body functions. Peas, corn, and sprouts are high in phosphorus, needed in body metabolism. Bananas, citrus fruits, and vegetables provide potassium, which helps nerves and muscles function. And sodium, which serves many functions, is found in many fruits, vegetables, and grains.

A group of minerals called electrolytes (chlorine, sodium, and potassium) are particularly important to cyclists. A lack of electrolytes will hurt physical performance and may even lead to heat exhaustion or stroke. Sodium, potassium, and

102 | save gas • go green • get fit

iron are lost through perspiration and need to be replenished by eating foods high in those minerals or by drinking special electrolyte replacement drinks and taking iron supplement pills.

Though cyclists need more vitamins and minerals to replace those that are lost through physical activity and perspiration, an excess of them does not increase health or fitness. Too much of them, in fact, can be unhealthy, or at least counterproductive to fitness.

DIET GUIDELINES

A healthy diet includes food from all the nutritional categories. Ask dedicated cyclists, however, and they'll undoubtedly emphasize one category in particular: carbohydrates. While fats and proteins can be reduced in your diet, carbohydrates should be increased to at least 65 percent of total intake, or as much as 75 percent for those who bicycle commute at high intensity. Proteins and fats should make up 10–20 percent each.

Whatever you eat, allow about three hours before heavy physical activity to digest a large meal. And be sure to eat another large meal within two hours of completing a heavy workout. Never try to deprive your body of needed nutrients in the interest of losing weight.

As important as what and when you eat is what and when you drink. In cycling, it's often said, "Drink before you get thirsty." A continuous, moderate intake of water, though, is much better than drinking large amounts at one time.

THE BEST FOODS FOR CYCLISTS

- Fresh fruits and vegetables
- Pasta and noodles
- Whole-grain breads
- Cereals
- Rice
- Tofu, soy products
- Low-fat meat, chicken, and fish
- Peanut butter
- Potatoes
- Nuts and legumes

FOODS TO AVOID

- Fatty meats and poultry
- Fried foods
- Whole-milk products
- Egg yolks
- Saturated oils and shortening
- Sugary foods and snacks

INJURY PREVENTION

The more you ride the better chance you have of suffering discomfort from time to time. Though not usually serious, any discomfort may make riding painful or develop into a worse problem if ignored. Sometimes the ailment stems from a problem with your form or with the fit of your bike. Other times it's just a matter of wear and tear on your body.

In either case, there are usually remedies—either behavioral changes or treatments—that can cure your discomfort, or at least minimize it. Whenever an ailment continues or worsens over time, though, professional medical help should be sought.

BACK AND NECK

Back problems are very common in society in general, and particularly prevalent in cyclists. Most often, the problem is a matter of poor posture—not only while riding but also when sitting and standing. People often roll their backs, which puts undo stress on the spine and lower back muscles, rather than keeping backs straight or arched.

Posture problems are remedied, simply, with better posture. While riding, your back should be completely straight. Practice pushing your belly out and toward the top tube in order to achieve a flat back. Off the bike, provide support for your lower back by using cushions and pillows and by remembering to sit up straight.

Sometimes, backaches afflict new riders because they are using unfamiliar muscles. Riders with excessive fat around the waist may put extra strain on their backs while cycling. On long rides, even trained riders can feel back discomfort from many hours of leaning forward. These pains should go away as lower back muscles are developed. Stretching and exercising both back and abdominal muscles will help speed the process; so will making sure your back stays warm while riding.

Often, improper positioning or bike fit can strain your back. Consider temporarily raising your handlebars to make it easier to straighten your back. For chronic back pain, consider switching to a recumbent bike.

Neck problems can also result from improper body position or a bike fit that makes you cramped. It can often be prevented by alternating your position regularly between upright, drop position, and out-of-the-saddle riding. If your bike has been properly fitted to your body, the most adjusting your bike should need is to slide the saddle back, raise the handlebars, or get a longer stem. Proper stretching and exercises will help strengthen neck muscles as well.

Ice packs, heat treatments, and light massage can help reduce pain and inflammation in the back and neck. Medications such as painkillers, muscle relaxants, and anti-inflammatory drugs can help as well. You may need a doctor's prescription for more powerful medications.

KNEES

The knee is a large, complex—and not particularly strong—joint, giving the dedicated cyclist plenty of opportunities for injury. Four bones, three muscle groups, cartilage (for cushion), fluid (for lubrication), and ligaments (to hold everything together) all meet at the knee in an arrangement that is not fully prepared to accommodate the stress of heavy pedaling.

Knee trouble can arise for a number of reasons. Improper saddle height or seat positioning can damage knees. When the seat is too low, knees cannot extend properly and may become cramped or strained; if the seat is too high, the kneecap becomes overextended. Improper foot position can also make your knees vulnerable; and problems with the bike itself—particularly in the pedals or cranks—could throw off your form. Ideal seat height will allow your knee to be almost fully extended at the bottom of the stroke, though not extended far enough to lock into place.

But even on properly sized bikes, cyclists necessarily put a lot of pressure on their knees. Pedaling is a repetitive motion that requires continuous bending of the knee joints and flexing of the surrounding muscles. Knees bend and straighten thousands of times over the course of a few miles; in time even mildly stressful pedaling will take its toll. Riding too much, too hard, or in too high a gear before your leg muscles are properly developed can strain knees and make them sore. Also, the limited range of knee extension puts more stress on certain muscles than others, causing an imbalanced muscle development and excessive friction between muscles, bones, cartilage, and ligaments.

The treatment is simply to take it easy. Realize your body's limits and respect them. If you experience pain, allow your knee to rest for a few days. Don't put any unnecessary pressure on it; ice packs can help, and pain relievers will ease the discomfort. Once the pain has dissipated, start riding again, but with less intensity. To prevent stiffness, be sure to keep the knees warm. Also, stretching the muscles around the knees—the hamstrings, quadriceps, and calves—will reduce the likelihood of knee pain.

If knee pain is not addressed at the earliest signs, more serious conditions such as tendinitis, bursitis, and chondromalacia can develop. Tendinitis is an inflammation of the tendons surrounding the knee, either below the kneecap or on the side of the knee. Bursitis is an inflammation in the knee that results when the fluid sacs that lubricate the joint (bursa) become irritated. Chondromalacia occurs when the inside surface of the kneecap and surrounding cartilage become worn down through excessive friction, resulting in pain and a grating feeling in the knee.

Again, the best treatment for mild cases of any of these conditions is rest, proper knee exercises, ice treatment, and anti-inflammatory drugs. Appropriate adjustments to seat height and pedaling form should be made as well. For advanced cases, an orthopedic doctor or physical therapist should be consulted. More involved treatment, perhaps even surgery, could be necessary. Chondromalacia, for one, is difficult to treat once it reaches an advanced stage. Through inflammation and pain, your body will alert you to any problems; just be sure you're paying attention.

The good news, though, is that under proper conditions, cycling puts much less strain on the knees than other physical activities that require running. The chances of seriously hurting the knee are significantly reduced when feet are on pedals instead of pounding on the ground.

SEAT DISCOMFORT

A comfortable bike seat will help reduce saddle discomfort. Many saddles now feature cutouts or grooves to avoid pinch or pressure on sensitive tissue. Seats should be well padded, smooth, and wide enough for your body (too wide, though, can make matters worse). Women's and men's seats are designed differently to better support different bone structures. Take some time to find a seat that fits your body and will keep its shape over long rides. While a seat that is too slippery can be dangerous (if you slide off), one that is not slippery enough will cause irritation. Look for a happy medium.

If you experience soreness in your seating area, adjust the saddle height or tilt. You may also want to check your riding position, and possibly raise your stem to ride in a more upright seated position and relieve pressure on sensitive tissue. Many cyclists experiencing sore butts blame the saddle, when it could be other aspects of your riding position that put weight on delicate areas.

FEET AND HANDS

Many miles of riding in the same position can cause numbness in the feet and hands. The most obvious solution is to change positions by shifting your weight, moving your hands, or riding out of the seat for a while.

Shoes that are too small, narrow, or tight can also cause numbness or even calluses and blisters. While some shoes need to be broken in, shoes that continue to cause discomfort after weeks of heavy use are simply not the right shoes for you. In addition, riding with soft-soled shoes can cause a burning sensation in the bottom of the feet; hard soles distribute the pressure of pedaling throughout the feet to provide more comfort. Feet also swell slightly during activity; your shoes should allow for adjusting during a ride.

Numbness of the hands is caused by handlebar pressure on the palms that cuts off circulation to the fingers. Numbness can usually be prevented by easing up on your grip and switching handlebar positions as much as possible. Bikes with drop handlebars provide at least three completely different hand positions, while straight handlebar bikes (mountain bikes) give the rider less choice. Adding bar ends to a flat handlebar will provide an additional riding position. Continued discomfort may require you to wear riding gloves or (if you already wear gloves) gloves with more padding. Padding on handlebars also reduces the road friction that causes hand pain and numbness.

The shocks of the road can take their toll on the wrists as well as the hands. Carpal tunnel syndrome, a nerve condition in the wrists that commonly affects typists, can also plague cyclists. Rest, better shock absorption, and a modified grip will lessen the stress on wrists.

SUN EXPOSURE

Hardly a problem faced by cyclists alone, sunburn must be dealt with by anyone who spends a lot of time outdoors. But because the wind cools cyclists as they ride, they often don't feel the sun burning down on them. That's why it's even more important for bike riders to prepare for the sun before they even venture outside.

The best way to prevent sunburn is to use sunscreen. Depending on your skin tone, it's best to start with a lotion having a sun protection factor of at least 30 or as high as 50 for particularly fair-skinned cyclists. Lotion should be waterproof and sweatproof. Apply it everywhere skin is exposed: face (including neck and ears), arms, and legs.

If a sunburn has already occurred, apply cream or lotion to moisturize and cool the skin. Pain relievers can ease the burn as well. Other than that, you just need to wait it out; most sunburns will subside within a few days.

CHAPTER 7

Commuting Safety

Many people don't commute on a bicycle because of perceived safety fears. The perception is far worse than the reality. Don't let exaggerated fear prevent you from enjoying healthy, money-saving, and environment-friendly activities such as bicycling.

That said, bicycling is not without its risks. Each year, approximately 700 people die in cycling crashes in the United States. Those deaths are tragic and unacceptable. But in a country of more than 300 million people that's not many, especially compared to fatalities of car crashes, gunshot wounds, workplace accidents, medical malpractice, tainted food, obesity, smoking, and alcohol abuse. Considering the life-extending health benefits of bicycling, it may be less safe to *not* bicycle. Sedentary lifestyles kill far more Americans than bicycling.

Many of the risks of bicycle commuting can be avoided or mitigated through proper bicycling technique, attentive riding, and street smarts. More than one-third of cycling fatalities in the United States are children under the age of eighteen; another significant share involve cyclists under the influence of alcohol or drugs; and another major share are cyclists riding without lights or the wrong way against traffic. If you are an adult bicyclist who stays sober while riding, uses lights when biking at night, and rides correctly, your risk of being killed while bicycle commuting are very minimal. This chapter will assist you in safely enjoying bicycle commuting.

KNOW YOUR BICYCLE

The best way to improve your bicycling safety is to simply bicycle more. If you are just starting out as a new or returning bicyclist, take your bike to a quiet street or park and practice riding. Get to understand how your bike handles: how quickly it stops, how quickly it accelerates, how it turns, how the shifting works, how the tires respond. Gaining confidence in your bicycle-handling skills will greatly improve your safety. If you are a new bicyclist, you might also consider enrolling in a bicycle education course, offered by many local bicycling organizations or government agencies.

PRERIDE INSPECTION

Many bicycle falls are the result of equipment malfunction. Keep your bike well maintained and you will avoid many accidents on your commute. Before you get on your bike to take a ride, it's important to give a quick look to check that all bike parts are tight, well adjusted, and working properly. At a minimum, many bicyclists do the ABC Quick Check: Air, Brakes, Crankset, Quick Releases. Make sure your tires are properly inflated, check that your brakes are good, confirm that your chain is in the chainrings and cogs, and assure that your quick releases on the wheels are closed. Assuming you don't find any problems, this inspection should take no more than a couple minutes. Any problems you find, though, should be addressed immediately. The following is a discussion of things to check more thoroughly.

DAILY TO-DOS

Check the frame. Most frames are strong enough to easily handle normal riding. But if you have a mountain bike and take it off-road a lot, you should check the frame for cracks and dents before (and after) you take it out on the trails.

Check quick releases. Depending on your bike, you may have quick-release levers on the seat tube or front and back wheel hub. Make sure these are locked and secured tightly.

Check seat. Seat tilt should be in the correct position and fastened tightly. It can come loose from hard riding, particularly off-road.

Check tires. Tires should be properly inflated to the recommended pressure, which is usually written on the side of each tire. Use a tire gauge to measure the air pressure. If necessary, inflate the tires with an air pump. Also, check the surface of the tires for worn-down tread, cuts, or embedded road debris (stones, glass).

Check wheels. Spin each wheel to see that it is properly centered in the frame and completely flat (called true). If the wheels look wobbly when they spin, they may need to be trued (or the hub bearings may need adjustment). Also, try to move the wheels side to side with your hand to make sure that they are secure and don't touch the brake pads. In addition, make sure the spokes are tight by moderately plucking them.

Check brakes. Squeeze each brake lever independently as you push the bike forward. The levers should activate the brake pads to press securely around the wheel rim and stop the wheels completely. Check that the pads are not worn down and make sure the rims are clean and dent free.

Check the cables. Inspect the entire length of brake and derailleur cables for any breaks or loosening, particularly at the mounting points.

Both the **pedal screws** and the **chainwheel bolts** tend to come loose over time. Feel for play in these areas.

Check the headset and forks. The headset should be sturdy and tight but turn smoothly.

Make sure headset bearings do not rattle. If you have a mountain bike with suspension forks, check that all fork bolts are secure. Push down on the handlebars to test whether the suspension works properly.

MONTHLY

Check wheels. Make sure the wheels are true. Spokes should be wound tightly and the rims should have no warps.

Check the cranks. Ensure they are tight and the crankset turns smoothly.

QUARTERLY, AS NECESSARY

Check drivetrain. Examine the chains and the sprockets for wear. Adjust or replace parts as necessary.

Check bolts. Confirm that all bolts holding racks, water bottles, or other accessories are snug.

RIDING CONFIDENTLY

Safe bicycling is not simply a matter of following the law. Many safety principles are not covered in traffic regulations but are important nevertheless. Like any vehicle on the road, bicycles can be perfectly safe or they can be extremely dangerous.

Remember a few basic concepts that will help you ride safely:

hand signals

left turn or merge

or

right turn or merge

or

stop or slow down

Speed kills. Going fast on a bicycle is thrilling. But don't ride at a speed beyond your capabilities. Keep your bike in control at all times. Don't sacrifice safety for thrills.

Be seen. Ride predictably, with traffic, where motorists and other road users can see you. Stay in the traffic lane, maintaining a straight line; don't move in and out of empty parking spaces. Never ride against traffic; wrong-way cycling is extremely dangerous.

Be heard. Communicate with motorists, pedestrians, and other cyclists. Use hand signals to indicate turns and stops. Use your bell or horn to alert others of your presence. Make eye contact with motorists to be sure they see you. Smile, wave, gesture, express gratitude when motorists yield the right of way. Show how much fun you're having on your bicycle and maybe some drivers will be tempted to join you in bicycling enjoyment.

Be assertive. Timid riding invites abuse. You have a right to the road. Claim it. Define your space. Don't be bullied.

OTHER SMART RIDING PRINCIPLES

- Be familiar with your route and know when you will have turns or intersections. Anticipate these and adjust your speed to make turns. Know where hazardous conditions may be.

- Understand your bicycle. Know your bike's stopping and turning capacities.

- Be courteous to others. Let cars and bikes pass whenever possible, and don't lean on stopped or parked cars.

- Don't ever tailgate a motor vehicle—a sudden stop could spell trouble. While following another bicycle closely (called drafting) has its advantages, it should only be done under specific circumstances, with the permission and knowledge of the other cyclist.

- Always check your bicycle for mechanical trouble before riding.

- Move quickly and completely off the road to check a mechanical problem you may have with your bike.

- Don't race on public roads.

- Ride in single file when biking with other cyclists, unless space permits riding abreast.

- Be especially careful riding at night, and don't ride at night unless your bicycle is properly equipped.

- Wear bright colors so you can be seen more easily.

- Carry some form of identification with you when riding, in case of an emergency.

- Help others when you see they are in need.

ROAD HAZARDS

Collisions with cars and other bicycles account for only about one-third of all bike accidents. That means there are plenty of other things to look out for when riding. While many road hazards won't cause more damage than a flat tire or a skid, some can cause more serious harm. The worst hazards knock riders off their bike or cause serious injury, even death. Be ready for anything: keep your head up, your eyes on the road, and stay alert at all times. Slow down whenever hazards are present.

A bicycle should be in excellent shape to safely and quickly react to unexpected occurrences. Brakes should be tight and tires cleaned frequently of the debris that accumulates on them. Carry a spare tire tube or patch kit as well in case sharp objects prove unavoidable.

One of the most common causes for a crash is an open car door. Cars parked parallel to the street may suddenly open a door into traffic. There are ways to avoid this though. For starters, always ride clear of the "door zone," maintaining a safe distance from parked cars. This may be difficult on narrow streets. Claim your space. A honking motorist is fine; at least they see you. If you must travel in the "door zone," slow down and anticipate opening doors. Look in vehicles to see if they are occupied; look into driver side mirror to see if a driver is present.

Following are some other things to look out for:

DAMAGED AND UNSAFE ROADS

- Potholes, particularly in winter and spring when they're most likely to form
- Loose debris from potholes, often lying near the pothole
- Metal plates, loose gravel, or other construction material
- Metal sewer gratings, which can catch bike tires if they are wide enough

Avoidance techniques: Slow down, check traffic, and safely swerve out of the way.

SHARP MATERIALS

- Glass, accumulates at the corners of intersections
- Gravel, particularly sticky bits from newly paved roads
- Twigs, thorns, pine cones, cactus spines, or other debris that has fallen from plants and trees

Avoidance techniques: Slow down, check traffic, and safely swerve out of the way. In addition, brush off tires frequently to keep sharp pieces from digging into them. If your bicycle commute route features much sharp road debris, consider upgrading to more puncture-resistant tires, lined with Kevlar or other protective material.

SLIPPERY SURFACES

- Ice, water, and mud, which make brakes less effective
- Leaves, especially when wet and newly fallen

- Oil slicks, which can be difficult to see and may stick to bike tires, making riding treacherous
- Painted street markings and pavement, especially when wet
- All metal surfaces, including manhole covers, railroad crossings, and bridge expansion joints

Avoidance techniques: If it is impossible to safely avoid slippery areas, drift through them slowly and smoothly. Ride straight; do not swerve, brake, jerk, or pedal until you are out of the area. Ride over metal tracks perpendicularly or, if you can do it safely, jump them.

FELLOW TRAVELERS

- Pedestrians, who can be unpredictable (watch especially for children)
- Wind created by fast-moving vehicles as they pass, which can throw you and your bicycle off balance
- Animals (squirrels, for instance, may dart unexpectedly)

Avoidance techniques: Ride in the street, not the sidewalk. Notify pedestrians of your approach with a horn, bell, or vocal warning, and give them time to get out of the way. Ride as far to the right as practicable and as far from high-speed vehicles as possible.

BEWARE OF DOG

When you come upon an unleashed and barking dog, don't overreact. Usually the dog means no harm and will lose interest as you pass. But if a dog is aggressive and begins to chase, you will need to take action. Try to either turn around or speed up to outrun it. While taking care to avoid a collision with the dog, don't let the animal distract you from the road. Firmly and loudly yell, "Stay!" or "No!" at the dog. If that doesn't work, raise your hand as if to throw something at it (but don't actually throw anything). As a last resort, spray some water from your water bottle into the dog's face. If you must get off your bike, use the bike as a barrier between you and the dog. If the dog's harassment becomes a regular occurrence, speak to the dog's owner or report the dog to authorities.

TECHNIQUES FOR RIDING SAFE

As discussed earlier in the chapter, riding a bicycle in traffic is not all that different from driving a car. Most of the same rules apply. The key is to become a part of traffic. Bicyclists are traffic—you have a right to the road. While some motorists believe bikes don't belong on the road, remember your rights. Take your rightful place in the streets through safe and competent riding.

AVOID TRAFFIC CONGESTION

Cycling in traffic is not dangerous if bicyclists are alert, know their capabilities, and follow smart riding techniques. But even for the most cautious riders, heavily congested streets are always less pleasant than bicycling on streets with no traffic. So avoid riding in heavy traffic whenever you can.

Take roads less traveled, even if they make for a slightly longer route. Quiet streets are not only safer, they can make the ride quicker by circumventing traffic jams.

If you must ride on congested streets, stay to the right, travel with the flow of traffic, and keep away from riding close to motorist traffic whenever possible. If the road has a clear and well-paved shoulder, use it.

PASSING

Because bicycles generally move slower than cars on the road, you will be passed more often than you pass. While cars approaching from behind cause much anxiety for inexperienced cyclists, you needn't worry; passing cars are rarely the cause of car-bike collisions. Whenever it is safe to let a car pass, do so. Sometimes, though, cyclists are better off holding up cars in the interest of safety. On narrow roads, for instance, squeezing right to let a car pass could send bikes off the road or into hazardous road debris. Ride close to the middle of the lane when necessary; if the car wishes to pass, let it switch lanes. This is the law in most states: Passing is allowed only when it is safe. Take the lane; control your space.

On those occasions when you need to overtake a car (or another bicycle), always signal your intention to pass, and pass on the left. Passing on the right isn't recommended, unless the other vehicle plans to turn left or the lane between the car and your bike is clear. Passing on the left, of course, means you need to leave the right side of the road for a time. That's okay. Just stay out of the car's blind spot as you pass and notify others as you approach. Then move back to the right as soon as it is safe.

NEGOTIATING SPACE

Switching lanes safely in traffic—a skill called *negotiating*—is among the most important riding techniques a bicyclist can learn. If you ever plan to make a left turn in traffic, you'll need to negotiate your way across the roadway to get into the proper lane. While leaving the safety and comfort of the right side to enter the main flow of traffic can be intimidating, negotiating is safe and easy when done correctly.

The first step in negotiating is to check behind to see if any vehicles are approaching. Try to make eye contact with drivers and use standard hand signals to make your intentions known and ask to be let in. If the driver slows down and indicates a willingness to let you in, nod or wave "thanks," then move gradually left into the lane. Continue glancing behind to ensure other cars do not enter the lane. If you must negotiate across more than one lane, simply repeat the procedure. As you gradually move left, check traffic twice for each lane, once before you enter on the right side of the lane and once as you move across to the left side.

If you find yourself in the middle of heavy traffic, unable to shift into the left lane, do not stop. Continue riding forward, even if that means you miss your turn (you can always turn back later). In high-speed traffic, negotiation is much more difficult and dangerous—often impossible. If traffic is moving too quickly for you to interact with approaching drivers, simply be careful and shift lanes when you can.

HANDLING INTERSECTIONS

Many of the trickiest traffic situations come at intersections, where vehicles coming from various directions meet. Be careful and alert as you approach intersections because there's usually a lot going on. If you reach an intersection and find a line of cars waiting—at the light or stopped in a traffic jam—you may be tempted to squeeze through to the front of the line. Unless it is specifically outlawed in your state, this is certainly your prerogative. Be cautious, though, and watch for cars that may be shifting lanes in the traffic. As always, be as predictable and as controlled as possible.

If you end up in front of a group of cars at a stop light, it's best to let at least one car go through the intersection before you. This will establish the flow of traffic and avoid a situation in which a car coming from another direction does not see you and enters the intersection while you are crossing. To cross the intersection as quickly as possible, shift your bike into a low gear before you stop at a traffic light or stop sign.

To make a right turn at an intersection, simply remain in the far right lane and turn when traffic conditions permit.

When proceeding straight through an intersection, move left to avoid getting cut off by motorists turning right. If a right-turn-only lane exists, shift left to the right side of the first straight-only lane. Once you cross the intersection, return to your path on the right side of the road. If the right lane offers a choice to turn right or to go straight, move to the center of the lane, cross the intersection in the normal stream of traffic, and return right once you are through. As you cross the intersection, be prepared to turn sharply right

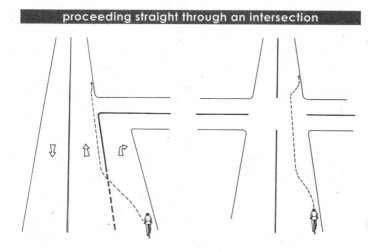

proceeding straight through an intersection

if a car from the opposite direction makes a sudden left turn into your lane without seeing you.

Left turns are more difficult and require planning long before you arrive at the intersection. When in doubt, simply get into the center of the correct turn lane. While this may slow traffic, it will ensure that you are seen and not cut off. If the left lane is a left-turn-only lane, move to the right side of that lane and turn wide to the right side of the cross street. If the left lane offers a choice to turn left or to go straight, move to the center of the choice lane and turn left into the center of the cross street before returning to the right side. If one left-only lane and one choice lane (turn or straight) exist, position yourself on the left side of the choice lane to make the turn.

Be sure to look both ways down the cross street and straight ahead before attempting the left turn. If you must wait in the center of the intersection while traffic from the opposite direction passes, turn your bicycle at an angle (45 degrees or less) to make yourself more visible to approaching cars. If traffic is very heavy, consider making the left turn as a pedestrian would. Remain right as you go through the intersection, then cross left on the crosswalk.

At a single-lane roundabout or rotary, ride in the center of the lane until you reach your turnoff, and watch traffic behind you before making the turn. At a multiple-lane roundabout or rotary, stay in the right lane only if you plan to make the first right. Otherwise, enter and ride in the left (inside) lane until turning off. Make sure the right (outside) lane is clear before making the turn.

turning left at an intersection

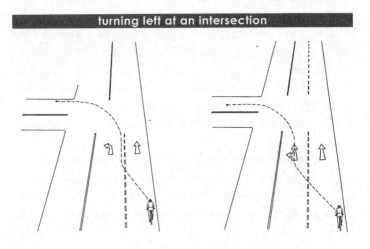

NIGHT BICYCLING

Nighttime cycling is somewhat dangerous even when you take the proper precautions. The two main problems are the facts that you can't see the road and that others on the road can't see you. Having a strong front headlight, a rear flasher, reflectors, and wearing bright colors (white and yellow are best), will do a lot to reduce the risks of night riding, but other safety precautions can be taken as well.

Try to ride only on well-lit streets that are well paved, hazard-free, and familiar to you. Stay out of shadows on streets, and completely avoid dark off-road trails, paths, or sidewalks. where pedestrians may be walking. In addition to being slippery, wet roads at night can produce a distracting glare from the streetlights that can impair your vision.

For the most part, apply the same traffic principles to riding at night as you would during the day. Keep in mind, though, that some drivers and pedestrians may not see you or your hand signals, so be extra cautious. Be sure you have plenty of room to make a turn before attempting it.

FREEWAY BICYCLING

Though bicycles are often restricted from them, highways with clean and wide shoulders can be relatively safe for biking. Where highway riding is allowed, bikes should remain on the shoulder as far right as is safe and practical. Because expressways have limited access, bicyclists only need to worry about breaks in the right shoulder at exits and feeder lanes. Where an exit lane approaches on the right, follow the shoulder into the exit until the exit completely breaks from the main road. Watch behind you for exiting cars; when the lane is clear, cut back to rejoin the highway on the right shoulder. If no traffic is approaching as you reach the exit, simply stay straight and cut across the exit. Or, if you plan to exit, follow the exit lane on the right shoulder.

Where a merging lane approaches on the right, watch for entering traffic. Shift right to the right shoulder of the merging lane as soon as possible, and avoid riding straight into the path of any entering cars. If you are entering on a merging lane, simply stay to the right as the merging lane joins the main expressway traffic.

THE PANIC STOP

Riding in traffic can be unpredictable. In an emergency, sharp and sudden stops can be necessary. A safer quick-stop technique—commonly called a "panic stop"—should be performed as follows: Shift your body weight toward the back wheel by sliding slightly off the saddle, and position your body low over the frame. Apply the brakes evenly and firmly on the front and back wheels, then gradually increase pressure on the front brake as you stop. Practice the panic stop several times in a safe location; get comfortable making this quick stop before you need to use it while commuting.

BICYCLING AND TRAFFIC LAWS

Most traffic laws are based on sound safety principles and have cyclists' best interests in mind. It's important to know those laws—those directed at all vehicles as well as those particularly for bicycles—before riding the streets. While specific laws vary from state to state, most general rules apply throughout the country. For information on bike safety laws in your state, contact your state's Department of Transportation, Department of Motor Vehicles, or your local bike shop.

The rest of this section contains an overview of the common bike-related traffic laws that may be in effect in your state.

- Obey all rules, signs, and procedures required of motor vehicles when riding on public roads. Compliance includes respecting stop signs, stop lights, speed limits, one-way streets, turn lanes, and other directions.
- Always ride in the direction of traffic. Inexperienced cyclists sometimes think riding against traffic is safer because it allows them to see approaching cars. But in reality, they are less visible and they put themselves at great risk for the most fatal kind of road accident: the head-on collision.
- Ride on the far-right side of the street. Slower traffic— no matter what vehicle—should keep to the right, and because bicycles are usually slower than cars, it's only logical they should be farthest right. Sometimes, however, moving too far right can expose bicyclists to other dangers such as the curb, road debris, parked cars, and pedestrians. To be safe, follow this rule of thumb: In wide lanes, ride just outside of normal traffic, a few feet to the right of passing cars; in narrow lanes, ride just inside the path

of traffic so that cars must move partially into the adjacent lane to pass.

- Pass on the left side when overtaking other vehicles in traffic, except if the other vehicle is turning left.
- Do not ride on limited-access freeways or other roads with high-speed traffic (over 50 mph) if restricted by state law. Bicycles are sometimes permitted to ride on the shoulders of these roads, if there are any.
- Do not ride on pedestrian sidewalks where bicycles are prohibited. While child bicyclists are encouraged to stay on the sidewalks, adults should avoid them. If sidewalk riding is allowed, watch out for people on foot, and follow pedestrian street-crossing rules.
- Stay off sidewalks unless local regulations allow it. Always yield to pedestrians whether on sidewalks, bike paths, or in the street.
- Use standard hand signals to convey any intention to turn or merge. Make signals early (100 feet in advance is safe). Be clear and deliberate, and repeat the signals regularly until you make the turn, merge, or stop. Signaling alone does not guarantee you will be able to maneuver safely, so continue to use caution.
- Stop for emergency vehicles and school buses just as you would in a motor vehicle.
- Do not hitch onto a motor vehicle in traffic. While some cyclists hitch on to move faster on the street, the practice is not only dangerous but also inconsiderate to drivers.
- Do not carry anything that obstructs your steering, hold, or balance.

- Do not ride with more people than the bike is equipped to carry: one person on a single-rider bike, two on a tandem.
- Keep at least one hand on the handlebars and your feet on the pedals at all times.
- Wear a helmet that provides proper protection. Though wearing a helmet is not the law in many states, helmets are extremely important because head injuries are the most common cause of bike-related fatalities.
- Bicyclists must be able to hear other vehicles as well as their own bike in case problems arise. Some states allow an earphone in one ear, if you choose to ride with a radio or MP3 player. Do not wear earphones in both ears while riding in traffic.
- Have a horn or a bell loud enough to alert nearby cars.
- Have a front headlight and rear reflector to see and be seen when bicycling at night.
- Use a specially designed child seat and child helmet if you ride with a child. Even in a child seat, babies who cannot yet sit unsupported do not belong on bicycles.
- Do not, of course, ride while under the influence of alcohol or drugs, including prescription medications that cause drowsiness or irritability.

SAFETY EQUIPMENT

There are hazards everywhere, and cyclists can't always depend on their riding skills to keep out of trouble. When a fall does occur, a helmet can literally make the difference between life and death. Statistics indicate that head injuries cause three-fourths of biking deaths, the vast majority of which could be avoided with a good helmet. Even a minor head injury can be devastating. That's why, in terms of safety, helmets are clearly one of the most important bicycle accessories you can have.

Helmets are not necessary to happily bike commute—in much of the world where bicycling is more prevalent, they are rarely used—but they do have a safety benefit. It is important to stress, however, helmets mitigate the consequences of a crash, they don't prevent a crash. Again, many of the risks of bicycle commuting can be avoided or mitigated through proper bicycling technique, attentive riding, and street smarts.

MATERIALS AND STANDARDS

While helmets won't guarantee that you escape a head injury, they will certainly make serious accidents a lot less likely. Of course, it's important to buy a helmet that's strong enough to protect your head. Helmets with expanded polystyrene liners—the same material used for packaging and coolers—spread out the force of the impact and offer the best shock absorption. Most helmets have a plastic or fiberglass shell around the hard foam.

Fortunately, shoppers don't need to be physicists to determine which helmets offer adequate protection. Each helmet should have a performance standard sticker affixed to the inside of the helmet (and similar information on the box if the helmet is packaged). Generally, each bicycle helmet sold in the United States must meet the U.S. Consumer Product Safety Commission (CPSC) standard. Other standards stickers you may see on helmets include the American Society for Testing and Materials (ASTM), which has standards comparable to the CPSC.

Another standard sometimes found in bike helmets is Snell standards B-95 and N-94, which are more strict but seldom used in bicycle helmets. Snell is short for the Snell Memorial Foundation, a private group named for racecar driver Pete Snell, who died in a crash in the 1950s, before protective helmets had been developed. Snell's standards, which cover racecar, motorcycle, and bicycle helmets, are a bit more strict than the others. Because Snell charges the manufacturer for certification stickers, helmets with Snell approval tend to be slightly higher in price but also slightly better in quality.

All helmets on the market—certainly any you would find for sale in a reputable bike shop—should satisfy one of the accepted standards. If you happen to come across a helmet that doesn't meet safety standards, drop it immediately. Don't even consider buying it, no matter what the price. Chances are it will not provide adequate protection.

FIND A COMFORTABLE FIT

While it's important that helmets are sufficiently strong, helmets also need to be comfortable. They should have soft padding inside in addition to the hard polystyrene protection on the outside. Try on a number of different styles and sizes until you find one that fits just right. If you can't find a comfortable helmet in one bike shop, go to others. Even if it means trying on dozens of helmets in a handful of stores, don't settle for one you're not completely sure about. Helmets that don't fit or irritate your head can become a major distraction and annoyance while riding—you may even be discouraged from wearing it.

A helmet that fits properly sits squarely and snugly, and covers the entire top of your head and upper forehead. Be sure to fasten it securely so it won't move or fall off under any circumstances. The helmet should have an adjustable chin strap made of a strong, comfortable material such as nylon with plastic buckles. Wash the straps occasionally to clean them of any dried sweat that can irritate the skin.

Never buy children's helmets in a larger size than necessary. It's just as important that helmets fit perfectly on kids. To avoid having to buy growing children a new helmet each year, buy a brand of helmet that comes with a few pads of varying thickness and use them to get the best fit as your child grows.

Fit is not the only consideration when looking for a comfortable helmet. A helmet should also be well ventilated to keep your head cool, using vents located just above the forehead to allow air to circulate. Many helmets can become almost unbearable on hot and windless days when you are climbing hills. Look for one that won't cause you to sweat excessively—some have pads that double as sweatbands— though how hot a helmet will make you can be hard to determine at first. If, while riding, you find you absolutely must take off your helmet, do so at your own risk and be sure to put it back on as soon as you cool down.

Comfortable helmets are also safe helmets. If they're too loose, they could slide around and block your vision, they may not protect you completely, or they may even fall off. If they're too tight, they could cause terrible headaches that would make riding dangerous and very unpleasant.

FASHION

Helmets come in many colors and patterns. While looks shouldn't be your primary concern, you may be more likely to wear an attractive helmet. For children, attractive designs and pictures on helmets are more likely to encourage wear. In addition, bright colors and reflective surfaces are more noticeable to motorists and other cyclists.

REPLACEMENT

Because helmet foam crushes on impact, helmets should be replaced each time they have been involved in an accident. Because the foam in bicycle helmets degrades over time, and sunlight, perspiration, dust, and rain all speed helmet deterioration, helmets should be replaced after a few years of use. For more information on helmet safety, contact the Bicycle Helmet Safety Institute at *www.helmets.org*.

EYEWEAR

Riding in the wind at high speeds, as many cyclists do, can put eyes in the path of all sorts of potentially harmful material: dirt, dust, sand, small pieces of gravel and glass, pollution, rain, mud, pollen, bugs, even the force of the wind itself. While a small particle is unlikely to cause serious damage to your eyes, it can very easily disrupt your sight, cause tearing, cause dry eyes, or otherwise distract you from the road long enough to put you in jeopardy. Though not absolutely necessary when riding at low speeds, glasses are often important to protect cyclists' eyes from any flying object that may cross their paths.

Sunglasses, of course, are helpful in protecting the eyes not only from particles but also from the blinding rays of the sun, which can be just as dangerous if road visibility is lost. Many sunglass brands offer frames with replaceable lenses, offering clear or darker vision.

Cyclists who normally wear eyeglasses can continue to wear them while riding, though they may want to get a pair of rugged sports frames. Those who normally wear contact lenses may opt to wear glasses instead. Riders who don't need to wear glasses to improve their vision should get clear, nonprescription glasses simply for protection. Tight-fitting elastic head straps keep eyewear in place, while loose straps that drape around the neck prevent the eyewear from falling onto the ground if it slips off the rider's nose.

Any eyewear you buy especially for cycling should be shatterproof and scratch resistant. It should have filtered lenses and provide proper protection from ultraviolet rays. Serious riders will look for eyewear that is lightweight and aerodynamic.

GLOVES

Gloves serve three purposes for cyclists' hands: shock absorption, protection, and warmth. Warmth being the least pressing concern, most biking gloves are fingerless, cut off just below the middle knuckles to allow hand dexterity (full gloves and mittens are available for cold-weather biking). Strong materials protect hands in case of falls. A padded fabric or gel lining in the palm provides shock absorption on bumpy rides that could otherwise cause muscle cramps, chafing, or numbness.

Most gloves are made of a durable, synthetic fabric, though a pair with leather or synthetic palms will be most comfortable. Velcro wristbands keep gloves on securely. To keep hands cool, some gloves are meshed on top for ventilation. Gloves should fit snugly but be flexible enough to allow your hands free movement. They should hold firmly to handlebar tape or rubber, which itself should be padded to decrease the effects of riding on rough surfaces. Gloves with reflective designs are particularly useful for night riding because they allow drivers and other riders to better see your hand signals.

REFLECTIVE MATERIAL

If you will be doing a lot of night bicycling, you may consider adding to your visibility with reflective clothing or ankle straps. One company, IlluniNITE, makes a range of reflective clothing, including jackets, shorts, vests, and gloves. There are many options for vests, which often feature a bright fabric and strips of reflective material. You can also acquire adhesive reflective tape to attach to helmets. There are many types of reflective ankle straps, which keep your pant leg out of the chain while improving visibility while pedaling. Many types of reflective clothing also improve daytime visibility.

IF A COLLISION OCCURS

If you are alert, savvy, and responsible when you bicycle, your chances of being involved in a collision are very small. However, collisions between bicyclists and other road users (motorists, bicyclists, pedestrians) do happen. Safety should begin long before the collision. Always carry identification, health insurance information, emergency contact information, a cell phone, and any allergy or healthcare issues. How you respond to a collision is very important. In many ways, the response should be similar to any crash involving cars: call for police, exchange information, get insurance information, examine damage, treat injuries.

ONCE A COLLISION HAS OCCURRED
- If you have been knocked to the ground, remain still until you can determine the extent of your injuries.
- Remain calm and avoid attacking—verbally or physically—others involved in the collision.
- Call for medical help or ask someone to do it for you, even if your injuries are minor.
- Call the police to report the accident, no matter how minor.
- Get the names, driver's license numbers, insurance information, and vehicle descriptions of others involved in the collision.
- Get the names, addresses, and phone numbers of witnesses to the collision.
- Ask witnesses and others involved to remain at the crash scene until proper authorities arrive.

- Cooperate with police when they arrive.
- Go to the hospital if your injuries require medical attention or documentation.

If you feel your rights have been violated, consult with an attorney who specializes in bicycling cases. You have the same right to the road as any other user. Never forget that. Your attorney should make an immediate investigation, obtain a statement from the driver, get witness statements, and take photos of the scene, the bicycle, and any injuries. If you think your damages are significant and you are considering litigation, it is very important to preserve evidence. Don't fix your bike or even wash the clothing worn on the day of the crash. It's all evidence that investigators can use to determine the facts of the incident, establish fault, and award damages. Even a grass stain on a shirt or shorts can be significant, as it can provide a clue about the motorist's speed and angle of collision.

IF AN INJURY OCCURS

In case you sustain minor injuries while cycling, it's a good idea—particularly on long rides—to carry a small first-aid kit with you. This kit may include:

- Adhesive bandages
- Nonstick pads
- Antibacterial ointment

- Pain-relief tablets
- Washcloth
- Ice pack

ABRASIONS

Minor scrapes caused by falling on the road surface are the most common types of bike injuries. Cyclists call such scrapes "road rash." Though road rash is usually not serious, it does hurt a lot. Protective clothing such as gloves, knee pads, elbow pads, and extra layers of clothing can help reduce the risk of abrasions. Here's what to do if you come down with a nasty case of road rash:

Clean out the wounded area completely with water, a clean washcloth, and antibacterial soap or an iodine solution. Scrub thoroughly to remove all the tiny particles of dirt and gravel that may have collected in the wound. Serious cyclists often shave their body hair, which makes cleaning these abrasions easier.

Treat the wound with an antibacterial ointment or other antiseptic and cover it with a nonstick pad or "second skin" product (a few varieties can be found in drugstores). Dress the wound only if it will come into contact with clothes or other objects. Otherwise, allowing exposure to air will hasten the healing process.

Ice the area as soon as possible to reduce pain and swelling. Scrub the wound twice a day with antibacterial soap and a washcloth to prevent infection and scabbing (scabs will harden and create more visible scars). Treat and dress the wound each time as directed above.

If a large area is lacerated, or if an infection occurs (evidenced by swelling, itching, or fever), see a doctor. You may need to take an oral antibiotic to fight the infection. Also, if you have not received a tetanus shot recently, get one from your doctor immediately.

BLEEDING

If a bike crash has caused you to bleed, apply direct pressure to the wound with a clean cloth in order to stop the bleeding. If possible, elevate the injury above your head until the blood clots. Clean the wound and dress it as described above to prevent infection. If the wound is deep or large, it may require stitches. In that case, or if bleeding continues, go immediately to the hospital emergency room.

SPRAINS

Wrists, knees, and ankles are the most common recipients of sprains from bicycle falls. A sprain is caused by damage to the ligaments around joints, and can put you out of commission (at least in terms of riding a bike) for anywhere from one week to a month or more. Put ice on the sprain to help cool the area and reduce swelling. If pain and stinging continues, or if a fever develops, the injury may be something worse than a sprain—it could be a fracture. Either way, it's a good idea to see a doctor.

FRACTURES

Wrists and collarbones are the most common types of bike-related fractures. If there is no visible sign of a bone break, your injury may at first seem like a sprain. The only way to tell right away if you have a fracture is to get an X-ray at the hospital. If the injury is indeed a fracture, the doctor will need to set the bone and bandage it. You may need to wear a sling or splint until the bone heals, which could take anywhere from two weeks to two months (collarbones heal quicker than wrists, though wrists can be less debilitating). Even after the doctor says it's okay to return to cycling, take it easy at first and stay off rough roads that can irritate the healing bone.

HEAD INJURIES

Head injuries are potentially the most serious type of injury you can sustain on a bike, and very high-impact head injuries can result in a concussion, a fractured skull, brain damage, or even death. However, they can often be prevented if the rider is wearing an effective helmet. If you have injured your head in a bike accident, get medical attention immediately. Allow yourself plenty of rest, even for the most mild cases. A head injury can be serious if you experience headaches, dizziness, vomiting, memory loss, or collapse.

HEAT STROKE AND HEAT EXHAUSTION

Heat exhaustion, and the more serious heat stroke, result when the body becomes overheated and cannot cool itself fast enough. In cases of extreme heat and dehydration, a heat stroke can be fatal. To prevent becoming overheated while you ride, carry a large bottle of water (sports drinks are good as well) and drink frequently. Don't wait until you feel thirsty or dehydrated—drink at least every ten minutes in hot weather.

If you begin to develop cramps or feel weak, dizzy, or nauseated, get off your bike and lie down on cool (shaded) ground. Elevate your head, drink regularly, and remain lying down until the symptoms go away. If you feel flushed and have a headache, dry skin, and a high pulse rate, it could mean a more serious heat stroke. If possible, wet your body and have someone call for medical help.

SPECIAL CONCERNS FOR FEMALE BIKE COMMUTERS

Most women and men are understandably concerned about their physical safety, and many women worry about criminal assault, especially in certain urban areas. Sadly, women are never entirely safe from verbal abuse, rape, abduction, or other assault. Women and men are vulnerable to attack no matter how they travel, whether driving, walking, using transit, or bicycling. Commuting by bicycle makes you no more vulnerable to assault than any other mode. In fact, often you are safer on a bicycle. For instance, if you approach a threatening situation, you can quickly reverse your direction on bike and escape a potential attack. Bicycling the wrong way against traffic is hazardous, but it many be the fastest escape route possible.

Female bicycle commuters should always take precautions against crime. That said, there is a difference between appropriate caution and paranoia. You shouldn't let fear prevent you from enjoying activities like bicycling that can greatly enhance your life. Among the precautions that bicycle commuters can take to improve their safety from assault:

Improve bicycle skills: Practice sprinting, jumping curbs, quick turns, and other escape techniques. Generally, the more confident you are while bicycling the safer you will be in all circumstances. Riding too cautiously or fearfully invites abuse, from drivers or potential attackers. Be assertive and confident.

Improve self-defense skills: Consider enrolling in a "model mugging" course, martial arts classes, or similar training. Carry pepper spray, which is available in lightweight, sports-specific containers.

Maintain your bicycle: Avoid having an unfortunate mechanical breakdown by keeping your bike in good operable condition. Make sure your tires are not too worn down.

Vary your route: If you travel regularly through sketchy areas, don't be predictable.

Be in control: Know your route and travel decisively. Be aware of your surroundings. If approached by a stranger, make eye contact. Just enough so they understand you would be able to identify them. Maintain and define your space. Don't ride too close to pedestrians or objects that might conceal an attacker. Don't be taken by surprise.

Use brighter lights: Use stronger lights that are bright enough to illuminate the street and reveal any potential threats.

Make noise: Carry a whistle, air horn, or other loud noise-making device. Carry a cell phone.

Your locks are weapons: If you can't avoid or easily flee a dangerous situation, your U-lock can be used as a club, and a cable lock makes an effective flail. Escape is always safer than confrontation; use your locks to fight back only as a last resort.

Trust your instincts: If a situation causes anxiety, turn around and leave. Get away to a place where you feel more secure. Heed your gut feelings.

BICYCLING SAFETY FOR CHILDREN

Many bicycle commuters are children, on their way to school or to visit friends. Bicycling is a great way for children to exercise, be outdoors, gain confidence, build self-esteem, practice problem solving, gain independence, and get where they need to go. Because they are often less familiar with traffic laws—and perhaps less familiar with how to ride a bike safely—children are at high risk of having a bike crash. For these reasons, it's particularly important to teach children how to maneuver in traffic.

As a bicycling parent, the best technique you can use to teach your children how to bike safely is to be a good role model. Wear a helmet, stop at stop signs and at lights, keep to the right, ride with traffic, signal turns, and exercise caution when riding. Teach them to be alert and attentive while bicycling on the street; children are easily distracted.

As with any bicyclist, children's safety will improve as they gain additional skills on a bike. Take your children to a park, bike path, or quiet street to practice their bicycling. Offer helpful suggestions. Make it a fun outing. As you teach your children to ride, make safety a primary concern. When they reach the age and skill level to venture out on the road, don't scare them. Encourage them to ride, as long as they can do it safely.

Many local schools or government organizations offer bicycling safety clinics, workshops, or rodeos for children. Find one near you and enroll your child. These educational opportunities can greatly improve your child's confidence and safety on a bicycle.

CHAPTER 8

The Trip to Work

You are ready to make your debut trip as a bicycle commuter. You have your bicycle. You have the necessary equipment. Your body is fueled and ready to go. You understand how to bicycle safely. You are excited in anticipation—and maybe a little anxious. There's no way to overcome that anxiety except by doing it. Just keep telling yourself that millions of people all over the world—including more than two million Americans—travel to their jobs on bicycles. You can do it. Let's go.

FINDING A ROUTE

A great route is a critical component of enjoyable bicycle commuting. It's possible your best bicycle-commuting route is the same as your usual commute by car or transit. On a trip to work, try to imagine how this trip might work as a bicyclist. Are there bike lanes? Is the route reasonably flat? Does your

route provide good shade trees, coffee shops, smooth pavement, quiet traffic? Do you see other cyclists—always a good
clue. If your usual commute has heavy, fast-moving traffic,
you will probably want to consider alternatives. There just
might be parallel streets that have less traffic and more comfortable conditions for bicycling. Maybe there's a bike path
you didn't know about. Consider all your options.

Spend some time before your first bike commute to work
researching your journey. There are many resources available
to assist you. Many communities create bike route maps,
showing bike paths, streets with bike lanes, high-traffic
streets to avoid, bridges that provide bike access, and other
amenities. To see if a bicycle map is available for your community, visit a local bike shop, contact your local bicycling
club or bike advocacy organization, or call your city or county
department of transportation.

The web is another useful resource for planning your
bike-commuting route. A resource such as Google Maps
offers street views and satellite images that might help you
understand the terrain of your commute. Bikely.com offers
ride suggestions submitted by thousands of bicyclists, one of
which might work for your commute. There may also be local
bicycling blogs or listserves where you can get insight on bike
conditions in your community. And many local and regional
transportation agencies offer online bicycling information.

Most of all, when choosing a route don't settle for the
first one you find. Though it may seem to be the shortest
and fastest path, you may discover better roads to ride. Try
several different routes to determine which is best. And even

once you have determined, beyond a doubt, the shortest path between two points, continue to alter your route every now and again just to get a change of scenery. After all, a little variety is the spice of life. And one of the great joys of bicycling is that you are part of your surroundings, not isolated behind glass and metal. You feel the air, smell the scents, hear the conversations, see things missed by motorists. Find routes that offer appealing scenery, friendly pedestrians, interesting shops, potential wildlife sightings, and stimulating terrain.

LONG-DISTANCE COMMUTE

When researching your bicycle-commute route, you may want to consider the transit options that serve your destination. If the distance seems challenging, especially if you are not presently an active bicyclist, you may want to consider a multimodal commute. Many bicycle commuters travel long distances by using transit for part of their route. Transit systems in many communities have become more accommodating to bicyclists in recent years, adding bike racks to buses, creating bike-carrying space on subway cars and trains, adding bike racks at transit stations, and even creating full-service bike stations at transit hubs, which feature secure, staffed bike parking and other services. Transit is also helpful to bicycle commuters in the event that they have an injury or sudden illness and can't make the bike ride home.

Many long-distance bicycle commuters also combine bicycling and driving on their multimodal commute. They may drive part of the way to their destination, park, and use their bicycle for the rest of the trip. Folding bikes, which can be easily stored in a trunk, are very helpful for this type of commute. Other multimodal bicycle commuters may drive to work, leave the car at the office, and bicycle home, and make the opposite commute the next day, bicycling to the job and driving home.

In considering your bicycle commute, don't let distance be a barrier. You can easily combine transit or driving with bicycling to make even the longest commute.

MAKE A TEST RIDE

Before you make your first Monday-morning bicycle commute to work, it's a good idea to make a weekend trial run of your route. It's better to discover any possible challenges when you aren't rushed. Maybe a hill you thought would take two minutes to ascend actually takes ten minutes. Maybe there's a dead end that isn't revealed on a bike map. Or maybe there's a bike lane you didn't anticipate. Make a weekend "try-out" ride, and then your first bicycle-commuting trip will be more relaxed. Ride in the clothing and carry the load you anticipate needing for work.

SECURING YOUR BIKE

You've arrived at work. Now you need a place to leave your bicycle. Sadly, employers in the United States are not very enlightened about bicycle parking. They aren't reluctant to provide parking for their employee's automobiles, spending thousands creating a parking lot or garage for staff car parking, and thousands more on lighting, maintaining, security, and insurance for these parking lots. Yet only one automobile parking space could be converted to create parking for ten or more bicycles.

Until your employer gets better informed about the value of staff bicycle parking, you will need to take responsibility for keeping your bicycle secure during the workday. Consider safety first when choosing a spot to lock up your bike. There are many acceptable places, from the impromptu locations such as strong metal gates and tall poles to the familiar bike racks to the fully protected indoor bike-parking facilities. If possible, try to leave your bicycle in a secure indoor location. Not only will this keep your bike secure from thieves, it will also protect it from weather. Perhaps you have enough space in your office to keep your bike there, where it will also become a conversation starter with colleagues and perhaps inspire others at your workplace to bike commute. Perhaps there is a closet or storeroom with space. The luckiest bike commuters work at organizations that provide secure indoor parking.

While regular commuters may want something that provides a bit more security (if it's available), most cyclists depend on what's available in the immediate vicinity. Wherever you decide to lock your bike, make sure it's safe for the bike and safe for everyone else as well. For example, don't chain your bike in a place where it will block pedestrian's paths. Besides being obnoxious, it may also be illegal.

Whenever possible, it's a good idea to park your bike in a location with abundant pedestrian traffic. Hiding your bike may seem like a good strategy at first, but it only makes theft easier for thieves who work out of the public eye. Fully protected indoor parking facilities such as bike garages and lockers provide the best protection. These may cost more than outdoor parking racks (which are generally free), but they also give you the most peace of mind if you leave your bike for long periods. Unfortunately, these more secure parking facilities aren't yet the norm at most workplaces in the United States.

Unless you leave your bike at a safe, supervised parking lot, always use a strong bike lock, preferably some sort of U-lock (see Chapter 5: Getting Equipped for more information on locks). You may also want to use more than one lock, such as a cable in addition to your U-lock. Redundancy is effective at deterring thieves, who may have the tools to defeat one type of lock but not several types of lock. And don't forget to take any accessories or easily removable parts with you when you leave the bike.

OTHER THEFT-DETERRENCE TECHNIQUES

In addition to securely locking your bike, there are other measures you can take to reduce the potential for bike theft.

Uglify your bike. Make your bike as undesirable as possible. Some cyclists remove brand-name decals or repaint the bike to disguise a top-of-the-line model as a piece of junk. Many bicyclists also put decals on their bike, both to express a message ("One Less Car," "I Bike & I Vote," or "What Gas Prices?") and to discourage easy resale in the event of theft.

Use a "beater bike." Leave your expensive titanium or carbon fiber bike at home, commute on a less expensive model. Many bicycle commuters ride "urban beater bikes" that are less appealing to thieves.

Make it unrideable. Many cyclists remove wheels and saddles to make it impossible for thieves to ride away on a bike. Even thieves who load bikes onto trucks may avoid those with missing parts; they don't want the hassle of finding spare parts when they can simply steal another bike without missing pieces.

Register your bike. Many communities offer bicycle registration through the local police department or other agency. Many states or communities also offer or require a bicycle license, which includes an adhesive label. There is also an anti-theft organization, the National Bike Registry, which also provides tamper-proof adhesive labels. These discourage thieves, who move on to unregistered bicycles that are more difficult to trace to the original owner.

Identify your bike. Many bicyclists use permanent markers to personalize their bikes, making them less appealing to bike thieves.

FIGHT BICYCLE THEFT

In addition to protecting your bicycle, there are additional steps you can take to discourage bicycle thieves in your community.

Report stolen bikes. Most times, police can't do anything to help you find a stolen bike, especially when it is unregistered. It may be either impossible to find the thief or too time consuming at a busy precinct. However, a large number of stolen bikes are eventually recovered so it's worthwhile to report a theft, just in case.

Never buy a stolen bike. Without a thriving market for stolen bikes, the huge problem of bike theft would not exist. To avoid stolen bikes, only buy from reputable bike shops. If someone offers you a great deal on a used bike, ask to see a receipt or registration. Without either of these, it's impossible to be sure the bike was not stolen at some point.

Record your bike's serial number. Every bike has a unique serial number, usually stamped on the frame below the bottom bracket. Record this number. If your bike is stolen, report it to help law-enforcement agencies recover your bike.

DRESSING FOR THE JOB

Depending on the distance of your commute and your intensity traveling it, you may need to clean up after your bicycle trip. If you commute less than three miles at an easy pace, you generally won't need much cleaning up. A washroom sink might be sufficient. If your trip is longer or you are pedaling briskly, you may need a full shower and change of clothing. If you are fortunate, there may be a shower facility at your workplace, with lockers for clothing. If there isn't a shower at work, there may be a nearby gym or health club that you could join, where you could shower after your commute. Many employers or health insurance plans provide financial support or incentives for health club memberships; check with your personnel office to see if there may be a health encouragement program at your employer.

Some bicycle commuters can make do without a shower, washing up in the bathroom, using some soap, a washcloth, a towel, deodorant, and cologne. Many bike commuters use moist towelettes.

If your employer does not offer suitable facilities, the best thing you can do is encourage others to start riding to work as well. You'll be setting a good example simply by commuting yourself. The more people who bike commute in your company the more likely the management will consider investing in better facilities.

EMPLOYER BENEFITS FROM BICYCLE COMMUTING

Fewer sick days, cheaper health claims. Biking to work provides employees with valuable exercise, which often leads to better health, less sick time, and reduced health expenses.

Better work productivity. Employees who exercise have less stress, better sleep, better focus, and are more alert.

Reduced absenteeism. Employees who exercise have better overall health, and enhanced mental health.

Improved employee morale. Employers offering diverse transportation options have greater employee satisfaction.

Less parking demand. Vehicle parking is expensive, with construction, maintenance, lighting, security, and insurance.

Talent retention. Offering diverse transportation options helps employers attract and retain the best employees.

Reduced turnover. Employers who appreciate workers' personal needs have less employee turnover.

Good corporate citizenship. Bike-friendly employers can gain significant public relations benefits, as businesses concerned about the environment, land use, traffic congestion, and the health and morale of their employees.

Source: Bicycle Federation of Wisconsin, League of American Bicyclists

WORK ATTIRE

If you've ever witnessed a man dressed in a suit and tie pedal down the street on a mountain bike, you know that some cyclists think nothing of simply wearing their work clothes while they commute. Perhaps they use an ankle strap to protect their pant legs, but otherwise they dress no differently than if they were driving a car to work. If you feel comfortable biking in work clothes—then wearing them throughout the day—that's fine; it's the fastest and most convenient way to commute.

Most bicycle commuters prefer to ride in clothes better suited for biking and then change into clean work clothes. To do this they need changing facilities (easy enough—any restroom or private office will do). They also need to pick out what to wear beforehand. Some commuters ride to work each day with their work clothes rolled up neatly and carefully in a backpack, pannier, or special bicycle garment bag. Others drive to work once a week and bring clothes for the entire week. Some never bring their work clothes home at all; they take them from work to a nearby dry cleaner and back again.

Once more, the type of job you have and your company's culture can affect the ease of your bicycle commuting. Commuters with jobs that require them to wear a business dress or suit every day have to work a little harder to transport clothes and to keep them clean and wrinkle free. Jobs where T-shirts and jeans are acceptable make wardrobe planning a lot easier. And no matter what your company's dress code, if it frowns on bike commuting as unprofessional or unbusinesslike, bicycle commuting can be more challenging. For people who commute to work daily, though, the extra planning is well worth it.

BE AN INSPIRATION

When you begin bicycle commuting, you may encounter some confusion among your colleagues, family, and friends. In the United States, the commute means driving alone.

Cars are the norm. Everyone does it, why change? It's simply assumed that because everyone drives, it must be unquestionably the best method of commuting. This misunderstanding may challenge your persistence as a bicycle commuter. You are stepping beyond the norm. You may hear a variety of questions or comments: "Why are you bicycle commuting?" or "Oh, you're *still* riding your bike?" or "Bikes are for kids" or "Can't you afford a car?"

As you persist with bike commuting, don't be surprised if those comments start to change. Your colleagues may start asking you how you got started bicycle commuting. They may ask for your suggestions on a suitable bike, or your help with planning a route. They may want you to meet them for their first attempt at bicycle commuting. You can encourage this attitude shift by being positive about your commute mode. Arrive at work with a smile. Talk about the birds you heard this morning, or the sunset you saw the night before. Mention how high you've noticed gas prices are. Don't be self-righteous or preachy; be a positive inspiration. Bicycle commuting isn't for everyone, but don't be surprised if you aren't seeing more of your colleagues joining you on the bicycle lane.

BIKE COMMUTING AND INCLEMENT WEATHER

Once you've started to bicycle commute, there's no reason to let rain, cold, or extreme heat keep you from riding. Around the world, people bicycle in hot desert climates to cold arctic climates. Experienced bike commuters have a saying: There's no such thing as bad weather, only bad clothing. With adequate preparation, you can bicycle commute year-round with little problem.

WEATHERIZE YOURSELF

Cyclists who ride in the rain are bound to get wet to some degree, no matter what precautions they take. But with the proper clothing, it's quite easy to stay relatively dry no matter how torrential the downpour seems.

Rainwear needs to be water resistant. While your winter gear should already be water resistant—because cold and wet tend to go together—you should also have some lightweight rain clothes to protect you from summer showers. The difficulty is in finding raingear that keeps you dry without making you overly hot. Fully waterproof materials, such as plastic laminated nylon, keep wetness from getting in but also block wetness (perspiration) from getting out. Synthetic linings, such as Gore-Tex and Ultrex, that are fused to nylon have tiny pores that allow perspiration to escape while keeping rain out. While not perfect, they're by far the most comfortable and effective water-resistant materials available. They'll also cost you a lot more than other rainwear. No matter how breathable the material, rain clothes should have some sort of extra ventilation.

Rain jackets should be tight enough so they won't cause unnecessary wind resistance, but they should allow room in the hood to cover your helmet (be careful of large hoods that limit peripheral vision, though). Underarm vents allow your body to breathe while keeping water out. Get a jacket that can roll up small enough to fit in a jersey pocket because you'll probably want to take it on long rides even when you're not sure you'll use it. For short-distance bicycle commuting in light rain conditions, a waterproof poncho or cape may work. This will protect your body and allow air to circulate around your body, keeping you from perspiring excessively. Ponchos or capes will offer more wind resistance.

Rain pants need to be snug and should have vents as well. They should allow enough room, though, for you to bend comfortably when riding on your drop handlebars. Gore-Tex or neoprene shoe covers are also available to keep feet dry. Or, you could simply tie plastic bags around your shoes— they're certainly no fashion statement, but as raingear goes, they're about as inexpensive and effective as it gets.

Because visibility is lower in the rain, it's even more important that rainwear be brightly colored or have reflective surfaces. And keep in mind, when the weather is warm enough and not too windy—and you're not headed anywhere special—encountering light showers while riding is really no big deal. If you do get caught without the appropriate clothing, a little rain never hurt anybody.

Between your cold-weather clothes and your raingear, you'll probably have an adequate windbreaker for any temperature. There's no sense in getting an additional nylon windbreaker when most rain jackets can serve both purposes. Recognize, though, that much of the chill you experience when riding is due more to wind than to temperature. Proper wind protection goes hand in hand with other specialty gear.

While some bike accessories are wholeheartedly recommended for any cyclist, not all of them are really necessary. Your need for a lot of equipment will depend on the kind of riding you do and how serious you are about it. To avoid weighing your bike down (and draining your wallet) unnecessarily, get just what you need and leave the rest on the bike store racks.

For extreme summer heat, the critical issues are protection from the sun and hydration. Many bicycle commuters wear lightweight, loose-fitting long-sleeve shirts to protect their skin, and sunscreen is very important. In hot conditions, you will want to carry additional water on all rides. If heat conditions are very challenging, you may want to adjust your work schedule to ride during the cooler parts of the days, in the morning or evening.

WEATHERIZE YOUR BIKE

During rainy and cold seasons, the most critical equipment you will need in addition to adequate clothing is fenders. The water that falls *down* through precipitation is not as offensive as the sloppy muck that splashes *up* from the road, even after the lightest rainfall. Fenders come in a range of widths and sizes. Some are quick attaching, to the seatpost or front fork, and can be easily removed when not needed. Other fenders are more securely attached to braze-ons on the frame and fork. Get the right size that covers your wheels and allows clearance for your tire width.

In snowy conditions, you may want to consider using tires with better traction. There are even bicycle tires with studs for icy conditions. In most communities, roads are cleared of snow pretty quickly, and within a day or two dry pavement is again present. One challenging element of bicycling during snow season is the sand and salt that many communities use to treat icy roads. Fenders will protect your bike from much of this slush, but you should wash your bike more frequently to clean off damaging salt brine.

In wet and snowy conditions, your bike will need more frequent cleaning and maintenance. Parts that are especially vulnerable to wet conditions include the chain and derailleurs. Refer to Chapter 9: Bicycle Maintenance and Repair for methods of cleaning, lubricating, and maintaining your drivetrain components. Wheels should also be cleaned more frequently, especially the rim surfaces, which are critical for braking performance. You will also want to use a bicycling polish on your frame to protect it from corrosive moisture.

WEATHERIZE YOUR RIDING

You will need to adjust your riding during periods of inclement weather. During rain or snow conditions, stopping and turning will be more challenging. Keep brakes and rims clean, to assure they work correctly. During rain, you will need to "feather" your brakes—pressing the levers several times rather than one firm pull—to wipe off moisture and keep brakes effective. Disc brake systems are more reliable in wet conditions. But stopping during rain will take longer with any brake system, as road surfaces are more slick.

During snowy winter months, roads may have more hazardous debris due to sanding and salting in icy conditions.

Plowed snow may narrow the road. There may also be more uneven pavement due to frost heaves and plowing, and possibly new potholes. Bike commuting during winter months requires more attentive riding.

Turning also requires more care during wet weather. Slow down and use extra caution when turning on any wet road surface. Conditions are most challenging during the first rain after a long dry spell, as accumulated oil residue on street surfaces adds to slippery conditions. Metal and painted surfaces are especially treacherous during wet weather; slow down and use extra caution when crossing train tracks, manhole covers, crosswalks, or other slick surfaces.

During extreme heat conditions, the primary concern is overexertion. Keep well hydrated, ride at a slower pace, and take breaks as needed. Find the shadiest streets, possibly the ones with ice cream shops en route.

NEED A CAR AT WORK?

Many people need a car as part of their work functions. This is a challenging feature for bicycle commuters. Many larger employers may have a corporate vehicle fleet, which could be used for daytime work trips. It may be possible to arrange to share a vehicle with a colleague. It may be possible that a vehicle is only necessary on certain days, and you can bicycle commute the other days. If your family has more than one car, it may be possible to leave one vehicle at your workplace.

In many larger cities in the United States, there are now low-cost car-sharing programs for short-term vehicle needs. Car sharing has long been popular in much of Europe, and car-sharing programs have been successfully introduced in American cities such as New York, Atlanta, Chicago, Austin, Portland, Washington, DC, and the San Francisco Bay Area. Many car-sharing organizations are run by nonprofit organizations or are locally owned. Zipcar is a national car-sharing operator with branches in many major cities, see *www.zipcar.com*. Many car rental companies also offer hourly rentals.

CHAPTER 9

Bicycle Maintenance and Repair

Bicycles are machines, and the fact is that machines need maintenance. That's the bad news. The good news is that bicycles are relatively simple machines—certainly when compared to an automobile, dishwasher, or notebook computer. Many repairs and normal maintenance can be done by even the least skilled mechanic. This chapter provides an overview of the most common bicycle maintenance or repair needs. For more complex repairs, visit a local bicycle shop.

TOOLS FOR BICYCLE MAINTENANCE AND REPAIR

The tools needed for bike maintenance and repair vary somewhat depending on the make and type of your bike. The number of tools you have will depend on how much work you want to do yourself. While all cyclists should know how to fix a flat tire and have the materials to do so, not everyone will want to undertake routine maintenance and more complex repairs. That's what bike-shop mechanics are for. However, if you are interested in bike maintenance and repair and willing to do a good job, by all means stock up on the whole spectrum of available materials.

Make sure you have all of the tools needed to do all the bike work you want to handle yourself. Don't try to squeeze by with a minimum of tools—you'll only make your job a lot harder. A well-stocked bike shop should have all the tools you need. Buy only quality tools from reputable manufacturers, and make sure the tools fit your bike (most bikes use European components that are sized according to the metric system).

BIKE TOOL SET AND MATERIALS
❐ Bike stand
❐ Screwdrivers: Phillips, flathead, and miniature
❐ Adjustable wrench and/or socket wrench
❐ Wrench set with sizes ranging 8–17 millimeters and/or three-way wrench with sizes ranging 8–10 millimeters
❐ Allen wrench set (also called allen keys or allen bolts) with sizes ranging 4–7 millimeters
❐ Spoke wrench (to fit spoke-nipple size)
❐ Pedal wrench or flat wrench, sized 13–16 millimeters
❐ Replacement bolts of various sizes
❐ Headset wrench
❐ Lubricant

❏ Chain remover
❏ Needlenose pliers
❏ Cable cutters
❏ Spare cable
❏ Crank and crankarm bolt remover
❏ Freewheel remover
❏ Cassette tool
❏ Tire patch kit
❏ Tire irons
❏ Spare inner tubes
❏ Replacement spokes
❏ Air pump and tire gauge

MAINTENANCE SCHEDULE

Any maintenance schedule will vary depending on how much you ride and how hard you ride. The following information is intended for cyclists who ride just about every day. If you only ride once a month, you certainly don't need to check your bike every week. But to keep your bike in the best possible condition, try to stick as closely (and practically) as possible to the schedule.

WEEKLY

• Clean your bike completely—particularly lights, reflectors, and wheels—with a damp rag.
• Check reflectors and lights for cracks, and check the batteries on your lights and computer.

MONTHLY

- Check the lubrication. If necessary, lubricate the chain, cables, and pivot points (on brake levers, shift levers, brake arms, and derailleurs) with a recommended lubricant.
- Check that all nuts and bolts are secure.
- Check that all the joints housing ball bearings are secure.
- Check all spokes closely for tightness.

EVERY 3–6 MONTHS, AS NECESSARY

- Clean the bike thoroughly and polish the frame finish.
- Clean the chain, sprockets, and derailleurs completely and relubricate.
- Check for chain stretch, and replace chain if necessary.
- True your wheels.
- Replace brake pads if worn and readjust brakes.
- Test gear shifting and adjust derailleur cables if necessary.
- Closely inspect tires, remove any debris lodged in the tread, and replace tires if they are cracked or badly worn.
- Clean and lubricate the tubes of your suspension forks, and replace any worn parts or seals.

ANNUAL, AS NECESSARY

- Take your bike into the shop for a tune-up. (Even if you're an expert mechanic, it's always good to get a second opinion. Another mechanic may notice something you missed.)
- Overhaul all component systems. Unless you are experienced in bicycle maintenance, this should be done at a bike shop by an experienced bike mechanic.

- Remove the seat post and relubricate it (be sure to mark the seat post height so you can reinstall it correctly).
- Remove the stem and relubricate it (be sure to mark it so you can reinstall it to the correct height).
- Clean the cables and replace if at all frayed or damaged.
- Replace cable housings.
- Check the pedals for damaged teeth and grinding bearings. Replace or repair pedals if necessary.
- Replace the tire patches and spare tube you carry in your repair kit if you haven't used them all year.
- Unload your bike's tool bag and home toolbox to check that all tools and equipment are in good condition.
- If you have suspension shocks and use them frequently, take your bike in to a bike shop for a suspension check (include it in your yearly tune-up).

CLEANING

Your bike should be thoroughly cleaned on a regular basis—either every week or every few months depending on your riding habits. If your bicycle commute includes some off-road riding, chances are good your bike will get dirty quite frequently. More than following any particular timetable, it's important to clean your bike as often as necessary. Clean bikes look better; but more importantly, they're safer. A buildup of dirt and other particles can quickly affect the performance of the brakes, chain, and other components.

To clean your bike, first get it completely wet with a sponge or low-pressure water hose (don't wipe dried dirt off the bike because you could scratch the finish). Then get a bucket of soapy water and a soft rag to further scrub the bike and wash away any dirt or grime from the frame and wheels. To wash the wheels, start at the hub and axle and work your way outward by wiping the spokes and rims. Do not use an oily cleaning product on the rims or the rim brakes will become ineffective. Remove any dirt, tar, or stones lodged in the treads. When you've finished, rinse all dirt and soap away completely.

The most important part of the bike to keep clean is the drivetrain (chain, crankset, cogs). Dirt or particles that get into the chain or bottom bracket can grind and wear down the parts. Short of disassembling the drivetrain and cleaning the parts individually, you can wash the area thoroughly with a brush and water or with special chain cleaning equipment available at bike shops. Loosen any debris from the chain-wheels, pedals, cranks, and derailleurs.

To clean the chain, spray or wipe it with degreaser, then run the chain through a wet, soapy rag (or chain-cleaning device) until all the oil and grease is removed. A good method to do this is to hold the rag around one part of the chain, then turn the cranks backwards to pull the chain through the rag. Once the chain is clean and dry, relubricate it with a light coating of a recommended lubricant and run a dry rag over the chain to remove excess lubrication.

After cleaning, inspect your bike closely to make sure all the parts are clean and working properly. Allow your bike to dry completely before you ride it.

BRAKES

To test the effectiveness of brakes, follow this procedure.

1. While sitting on the bike, coast moderately on a flat surface at five miles per hour (be sure there's no traffic).
2. Squeeze tightly on the brake lever that operates the front brake. If the rear wheel feels like it is lifting off the ground slightly, then the front brake is adequate. If not, the brake may need to be adjusted.
3. Repeat step 1.
4. Squeeze tightly on the brake lever that operates the rear brake. If the rear wheel skids slightly, brake pressure is adequate (too much skid could mean the tire tread is worn). If there is no skid or you feel a slow response, the brake may need to be adjusted.
5. If either brake has not performed adequately, check to make sure the levers, brake arms, and cables are pulling properly. Also check that rims are clean and dry.

BRAKE-CABLE ADJUSTMENT

If the brake is properly positioned around the wheel and the brake pads are making contact perfectly on the rim, any further brake adjustments you may need to make will likely involve tightening the brake cable. Follow these steps:

1. Loosen the locknut where the cable connects to the brake levers.

brake cable adjustment

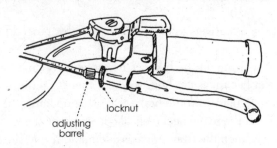

locknut

adjusting
barrel

2. Turn the adjusting barrel in the desired direction. It will be located either next to the locknut or near the rim brake itself. If the brakes are too tight (the wheels squeak while riding or rub against the brake pads), loosen the cable. If the brakes are not tight enough (insufficient breaking), tighten the cable.

3. When you have turned the adjusting mechanism to the proper point, the brake pads will be at an optimum distance from the wheels, the point at which they don't rub the wheel when at rest but brake effectively when the lever is squeezed (a few millimeters is good). With perfectly adjusted brakes, the brake levers will only need to be pulled a short distance to stop the bike.

4. Retighten the locknut while making sure not to turn the adjusting barrel.

BRAKE CENTERING

If your rim brakes are not properly centered, one brake pad will rest closer to the wheel than the other, rubbing the tire.

To readjust their position, take the following steps:

1. Many brakes have a small screw on top of the brake arms for centering the brakes. Turning the screw to make fine-tune adjustments will often center the brakes properly. If more adjusting is needed, continue to step 2. Note: Cantilever brakes may also have a small centering screw on each brake arm. However, since cantilever brake arms work independently of each other, the problem can usually be fixed by adjusting the distance between the brake pads and the wheel.
2. Use an Allen or flat wrench of proper size to turn the mounting bolt, which attaches the brakes to the fork. Turn the bolt away from the brake pad that is too close to the wheel. The bolt should be tight and difficult to turn, but only a slight adjustment is necessary.
3. When the brakes are properly centered, test them by flexing them. If they do not remain centered afterward, adjust the mounting bolt further, overcompensating if necessary, until the brakes remain properly centered.
4. Tighten the mounting bolt so it does not fall out of center.

WHEELS AND TIRES

To do most repairs and maintenance on the wheels and tires, you'll first need to know how to remove them from the bike and reinstall them.

FRONT WHEEL

Nearly all quality bikes have a quick-release lever on the front wheel hub that makes front wheel removal easy. No tools are needed. The quick-release mechanism holds the hub and axle on the fork. Simply push the lever forward to open the release (it should always point back when locked) and pull the wheel out. Another release lever, either on rim brake arms or near the brake levers, will enable the tire to slide out between the brakes (cantilever brake cables will unhook). To reinstall the front wheel, simply put the wheel back into the fork dropouts, center the wheel using the adjusting nut, and close the quick-release lever by pulling it back tightly. Close the brake release as well (or reattach the cantilever cables), and check the brakes to make sure they're properly adjusted.

If the bike does not have a quick-release front wheel, unscrew the nuts at the hub until the wheel comes loose. If the brake pads are too close to allow the tire to slide through, you may need to deflate the tires (of course, that won't be necessary if the tire is already flat). To reinstall the wheel, put it back into the fork slots, center it, and tighten the hub nuts. Reinflate the tires.

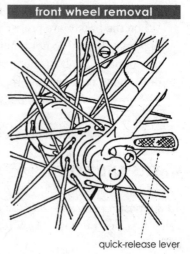

front wheel removal

quick-release lever

REAR WHEEL

Rear wheel removal and installation is a little more complicated. To remove the rear wheel, do the following.

1. While turning the pedals, shift the gears so the chain rests on the smallest cog and smallest chainwheel.
2. Release the rear brake arms, using the lever provided, to allow the tire to slide out. With cantilever brakes, squeeze the brake arms in and then unhook the transverse cable. This will open the arms wide enough to remove the tire.
3. If the wheel has a quick-release lever, open the lever to release the wheel. If there is no quick-release lever, unscrew the hub nuts until the wheel is released.

rear wheel removal

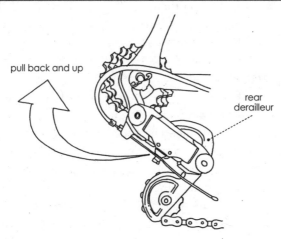

pull back and up

rear
derailleur

4. Pull the rear derailleur back and up to remove the chain from the rear wheel cog.
5. Pull the wheel out of the dropouts and away from the bike.

TO INSTALL THE WHEEL, FOLLOW THESE STEPS

1. The gear should still be set on the smallest chainwheel (and smallest cog if it was present), and the brake arms should still be released from the removal procedure.
2. Pull the rear derailleur back and up.
3. Move the wheel into position so the axle fits into the dropouts and the wheel is centered on the frame. The chain should come to rest on the smallest freewheel cog.
4. Close the quick-release lever or tighten the hub nuts to secure the wheel in place.
5. Restore the brakes to their position near the wheel. Test the brakes to make sure they are properly adjusted and the brake pads meet the rim.
6. Spin the wheel to ensure it is properly centered and doesn't rub against the brake pads.

FLAT TIRE REPAIR

If you only learn one bicycle repair procedure, make it this one. Flat tires are common and they can make riding dangerous or impossible. The procedure is quick and easy if done right. If you carry with you the necessary equipment (and you should!), tire repairs can be made on the side of the road (safely away from traffic) as well as at home. Have a tire repair kit or spare innertube, three tire irons (or tire levers), a spare tube, and an air pump with you whenever you ride.

Practice flat repair at home in good lighting. Fixing your first flat tire on the side of the road in the dark at night or during a rainstorm will not be fun. Carry a spare innertube for fast roadside repair, and patch the punctured innertube in the comfort of your home. Carrying a pair of latex gloves to wear when repairing a flat tire will make cleanup a snap. Dispose of soiled gloves properly. You could also use moist towelettes to clean up after a flat repair—also dispose of properly after use. To fix a flat tire:

1. Inspect the flat tire to determine, if possible, where the flat has occurred. If you can see any sharp object that has punctured the tire, carefully remove it and mark the spot.
2. Remove the wheel from the bike (follow the procedure in the previous section) and lay the bike on its left side (the side without the chain).
3. Deflate the remaining air from the tire by depressing the air valve or pin.
4. Wedge one of the tire irons (levers) between the tire and rim, a few inches away from the valve. Pull the lever down

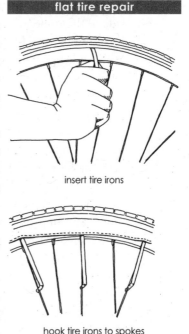

flat tire repair

insert tire irons

hook tire irons to spokes

to pry the tire bead over the rim, then hook the opposite end of the lever onto a spoke to hold it in place.

5. Repeat step 4 with a second tire iron, inserted a few inches away from the other tire iron.

6. If necessary, repeat step 4 again with a third tire iron, inserted a few inches away from the other irons.

7. Once the bead has come loose from the rim, use the tire irons to pry the entire side of the tire off the rim. Or, you may be able to do it with your hands. It is not necessary to remove the entire tire from the rim unless you detect a problem with the tire. Otherwise, leave one side of the tire on the rim.

8. Reach under the tire and pull out the innertube. Begin at the side opposite the valve, and remove the valve last by pushing it through the valve hole.

9. Locate the puncture. If you previously marked the tire (step 1), the innertube puncture should correspond to the mark. If not, inflate the tube partially and squeeze it. Listen to where air escapes or try to feel it with your hand or face. If that doesn't work, wet the tube with water and look for where a bubble forms when air escapes (dry the tire before repairing it). There may be more than one hole, so check the entire tube even if you've already found one puncture.

10. If you did not find any sharp objects in the tire in step 1, go back now and check the area of the tire that corresponds to the innertube puncture. Look for what might have caused the puncture and make sure you remove it from the tire.

11. If you have a spare innertube with you, use it. It's easier to replace the tube than to repair it, particularly when you are out on a ride. If you want to reuse the punctured tube, take it home and repair it later at your own convenience, then use it as your spare tube (make sure it works). If the tear is larger than ½", it cannot be repaired and must be replaced. To install a spare tube, skip to step 16. However, if you must repair the punctured tube using a repair kit, continue with the next step.

12. Find a patch from your repair kit that will cover the hole.

13. Use the scraper or sandpaper in the patch kit to roughen the area of the tube around the puncture. Scrape an area slightly larger than the size of the patch you will use.

14. Apply a thin, even film of rubber glue (from the patch kit) to the scraped surface and let it dry for a few minutes.

15. Remove the backing from the patch and, with the adhesive side down, carefully lay the patch over the scraped area. Press down on the patch to ensure a smooth and tight stick. Hold it for 1 minute.

16. Inflate the tube partially until it begins to take shape (if the tube has been repaired, make sure no air is leaking).

17. Insert the valve into the valve hole on the rim, then carefully insert the rest of the tube into the tire and around the rim without twisting the tube.

18. Use your hands to lift the tire bead back onto the rim (using irons may repuncture the tube). Make sure the tube is not pinched by the tire at any point. If necessary, deflate the tube to make reinstallation of the tire easier.

19. Inflate the tube fully with a hand pump as you check that the tire is centered on the rim, the bead is in the proper position, and the tube has not been pinched.

20. Replace the wheel on the bike (see directions in previous section).

SPOKE REPLACEMENT

If a spoke breaks while riding, it will send your wheel out of true and may make riding difficult and unsafe. While it's difficult to make your bike completely true again without spending a good deal of time—and without experience in truing wheels—replacing the spoke immediately will help stabilize any wheel problems until you can get your bike into the shop. To replace the spoke, follow these steps.

1. Get a replacement spoke that is exactly the right length. If you buy replacement spokes to carry with you, make sure they fit your bike.

2. If the replacement spoke is the same gauge (thickness) as the broken spoke, use a spoke wrench to unscrew the spoke nipple (which sticks out of the rim bottom) and release the spoke.

   If the new spoke is not the same gauge as the old, you will not be able to reuse the nipple. Instead, remove the tire from the rim in order to replace the nipple with one that fits the new spoke (always buy spokes and matching nipples together). Once the new nipple is in place, complete steps 3–5 and then replace the tire as explained in the previous section.

3. Thread the new spoke through the hole in the hub flange, exactly as the broken spoke was threaded. If the spoke is on the rear wheel, you will first need to completely remove the freewheel or cassette before you can slide the spoke through the flange. This will require a lot more work, but it is a necessary step.

4. Slide the end of the spoke into the nipple.

5. Turn the nipple until the spoke catches and tightens. Continue screwing in the spoke until a proper spoke tension is achieved. Do not screw the spoke in too far, or it may protrude into the rim and puncture the innertube.

WHEEL TRUING

Truing wheels is like tuning an instrument; most people can do it with experience and practice, while some people will never get it right. The best way to get your wheels perfectly trued without a lot of hassle is to take them to a bike shop. But for those who are determined to do their own bike repairs (and are willing to chance really messing up their wheels), the following explains the basics of wheel truing. Take your time the first few tries, and practice on an old rim that you no longer use. As you become more experienced, wheel truing should become much easier and quicker.

1. Completely remove the tire and innertube from the wheel.

2. Replace any broken or missing spokes exactly as they were originally arranged.

3. Tighten the spokes until all the spokes on each side of the wheel have the same tension. Equally tense spokes will

make the same musical tone when plucked. If you don't have an ear for music, estimate equal tension through the resistance of the spokes when plucked.

4. Using a repair stand to elevate the bike, reinstall the wheel without replacing the tire. The rim should rest between the brake pads.

5. Check for warps both side to side (laterally) and up and down (radially). To see lateral warps, stand directly in line with the wheel (in front of the front wheel or in back of the rear wheel) and spin the wheel. A laterally true wheel

wheel truing

tighten

loosen

radial truing

rim will remain exactly the same distance from the brake pads at all times. To see radial warps, stand to the side of the wheel as you spin it. A radially true wheel will be a perfect circle and always run parallel to the brake pads. The wheel will not have any humps or dips in the rim.

6. Locate any spots where the wheel warps. Mark these spots by holding a felt marker close to the rim and spinning the wheel. Only the warped spots will rub against the tip of the marker.

7. Tighten or loosen the spokes in the warped areas to eliminate the warps. If the rim warps laterally to the right side, tighten the spokes that connect to the left flange while loosening the spokes connected to the right flange. Do the opposite for warps to the left side. If the rim warps radially to create a hump, tighten the adjacent spokes (both on the right and left flanges) appropriately. Loosen the area spokes if the rim dips below true.

8. After adjusting the spokes, check that they are stretched and secured in the wheel by squeezing sets of parallel spokes together.

9. Repeat steps 5–8 until all the warps have been eliminated and the wheel is completely true.

DERAILLEURS AND FREEWHEEL

Both front and rear derailleurs have a pair of stop screws that regulate chain travel. One stop screw controls the amount the derailleur moves in (toward the wheel) and the other controls the derailleur's outward movement (away from the wheel). If the derailleur's range of motion is not sufficient to move the chain from the smallest sprocket to the largest sprocket, the stop screws need to be adjusted. Use an allen key or a screwdriver (depending on the type of stop screws) to turn the appropriate stop screw the amount necessary to allow full movement in the derailleur. Make small adjustments as you test the shift levers (the rear wheel must be elevated and the pedals turning to shift levers). Be sure you don't overadjust the screws. This will cause the derailleur to carry the chain entirely off the chainwheels.

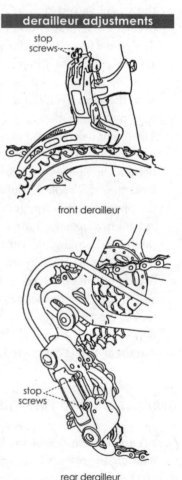

derailleur adjustments

stop screws

front derailleur

stop screws

rear derailleur

There are a number of reasons why derailleurs may not shift the chain properly between sprockets. First, the derailleur may have been knocked out of alignment by a fall or hit. If that's the case, the derailleur will need to be bent back into proper alignment with the sprockets. Beyond that, incomplete or improper shifting is likely the result of either a poorly adjusted derailleur or too much slack in the derailleur cables.

CABLE TIGHTENING

If you have determined that the stop screws are properly adjusted and the derailleur has an adequate range of sideways motion, you may need to tighten the derailleur cable. Some bikes have an adjusting barrel near the shift levers, similar to the adjusting barrel on the brake cable. If so, turn the barrel to tighten and eliminate any excess slack in the cable. If there is no adjusting barrel, you will need to unscrew the bolt on the derailleur that holds the cable and pull the cable taut by hand. Once the cable is taut, retighten the screw.

SADDLE AND SEAT POST

quick-release
seat post adjustment

If the seat post has a quick-release lever, follow these steps to make adjustments.

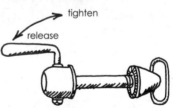

1. Turn the lever to loosen the seat post.
2. Holding onto the seat, slide the seat post up or down to set it in the proper position.
3. Holding the seat in place with one hand, turn the lever to secure the seat post.

If your seat post does not have a quick-release lever, follow these steps to make adjustments.

1. Use an allen key or wrench to loosen the seat-post bolt.
2. Holding onto the seat, slide the seat post up or down to set it in the proper position.
3. Holding the seat in place with one hand, firmly retighten the seat-post bolt to secure the seat post.

FORE-AND-AFT ADJUSTMENT AND SEAT-ANGLE ADJUSTMENT

Both the fore-and-aft position and the angle of the seat are governed by the same bolt or bolts, located underneath the seat. To make adjustments, follow these steps.

1. Unscrew the bolt or bolts with a wrench or screwdriver until the seat loosens from the seat post.
2. To change fore-and-aft position, slide the seat forward or backward. To alter the seat angle, tilt the seat up or down.
3. Holding the seat in the desired position with one hand, firmly retighten the bolt or bolts until the seat is secure.

HANDLEBARS AND STEM

Most handlebars are held in the stem by a binder bolt or bolts. Many older stems have a single bolt, which means the handlebar must be removed by sliding through the stem.

Most newer stems have two or four bolts holding the handle-bar. This enables the handlebars to be lifted straight off the stem as opposed to slid out from the side.

HANDLEBAR ADJUSTMENT

To adjust handlebar position, follow these steps.

1. Use a wrench or allen key to loosen the bolt or bolts that hold the handlebars in the stem.
2. Adjust the handlebar angle by turning the handlebars up or down as needed.
3. Holding the handlebars in place, firmly retighten the bolt or bolts until the handlebars are held securely in place.

STEM ADJUSTMENT

To adjust the stem, follow these steps.

1. Holding the bike firmly in place, loosen the stem bolt using a wrench or allen key.
2. Adjust the stem height by slid-ing it up or down into the head tube. Make sure the handle-bars remain centered and straight relative to the frame.
3. Holding the adjusted stem in position, retighten the stem bolt until the stem is held securely in the head tube.

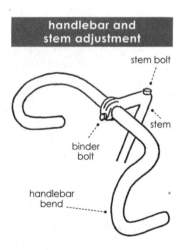

handlebar and stem adjustment

stem bolt

stem

binder bolt

handlebar bend

SPROCKETS AND CHAIN

Check the sprockets on your crankset or rear freewheel/cassette occasionally for damage and wear. Like wheels, sprockets should be true. If sprockets appear to wobble as they turn, they may have been bent in a fall. Even slightly bent sprockets may not catch the chain properly or may cause undue wear on the chain. While it's possible to repair a bent sprocket yourself by banging it back into shape with a hammer, you're just as likely to damage it as to fix it. Your best bet is to take your bike into the bike shop for sprocket repair or replacement.

A worn chain is the most common cause of worn sprockets. Chains that have been stretched will not fall precisely between the sprocket teeth. Over time, the chain will wear down the sprocket teeth on one side, causing the sprocket teeth to deform into a wave shape. The only way to prevent excessive wear on the sprockets is to replace your chain before it becomes stretched. Once a sprocket becomes worn it must be replaced.

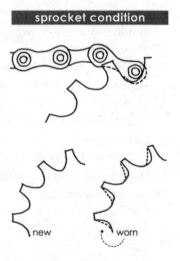

sprocket condition

new   worn

Use sprocket or freewheel/cassette removers to pull a sprocket off. If the sprockets on your freewheel/

cassette or crankset cannot be removed individually, you may need to replace the entire set of sprockets. To avoid replacing a complete set of sprockets, it's best to have individually removable sprockets. This way you'll only need to replace those that are more susceptible to bending (outside sprockets) and wear (small sprockets).

CHAIN LUBRICATION

Whenever your chain starts to squeak or feel dry (every 200 miles or so) you will need to relubricate it. Check lubrication regularly by touching the chain lightly with your finger or a rag. If little oil or grease comes off, the chain probably could use some more lubrication. It is also necessary to relubricate the chain whenever you have cleaned or replaced the chain.

A drip lubricant will create the least mess and ensure that the correct part of the chain is lubricated. Drip the lubricant lightly and evenly onto the individual roller pins of the chain. Be very careful not to get any lubricant onto the spokes or rims because lubricant could make the brakes unworkable. Use a rag to wipe any excess lubricant off the chain and chain stay.

CHAIN REMOVAL AND REINSTALLATION

To replace the chain or to clean it completely, you will need to remove it from the bike. Many chains have a master link that easily comes undone. On some chains, it is necessary to remove one of the pins that holds the chain links together. To do this, you'll need a chain remover or rivet extractor.

Extracting a pin from the chain may ruin the pin, so make sure you have a replacement pin to take its place. Some chains are easier to undo than others; higher-quality chains with special high-tension links tend to be more susceptible to damage. Be careful not to damage the links while extracting the pin. To remove the chain, follow these steps.

1. Shift gears so the chain rests on the smallest chainwheel and smallest cog.
2. Align the chain remover so that the chain runs through the tool and one of the pins is in line with the punch screw.

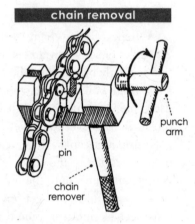

chain removal

punch arm

pin

chain remover

3. Screw the punch arm into the pin and push it through the chain links until the links come undone. Try not to push the pin all the way through; leave it sticking out the other side.
4. Retract the punch arm to release the chain links.
5. Slowly turn the pedals as you pull the chain free of the drivetrain.

When you reinstall the chain, it's a good idea to put it back on inside out to switch the side that gets worn next. To reinstall the chain, follow the following steps on the facing page:

1. Lay the unattached chain onto the smallest chainwheel and smallest cog, then weave it through the derailleur wheels.
2. Reconnect the end links at the bottom of the chain run. The extracted pin should be sticking out to the right, away from the bike. Hold the links in position while you set the chain tool in place around the link.
3. Screw the punch arm into the extracted pin to push it back into the chain. Continue twisting the arm until the pin returns to its original position.

CHAIN MAINTENANCE

Under stress, chain links become slightly stretched (actually, the metal around each pin wears down) and no longer thread smoothly onto the sprockets. In extreme cases, chains start to skip sprocket teeth, causing a harsh crunch sound during heavy pedaling. Replacing the chain every few thousand miles ensures the chain remains the proper length and the sprockets don't become worn.

To test the chain for wear, try to lift the links off the chainwheel. If the chain does not lift, there is no need to replace the chain. If, however, you can lift the chain off the chainwheel even a few millimeters, it should be replaced. If the chain has worn to that point, chances are good some of the sprockets will need to be replaced as well. There are also chain measurement tools, which can be used to test chain stretch.

Bicycling Beyond the Trip to Work

There are many ways to enjoy bicycles beyond healthy and economical commuting. Millions of people across the United States enjoy bicycling for recreation, touring, and competition. As you begin bicycle commuting, you may experience some sore muscles in addition to joy. As you continue with bike commuting, your fitness will gradually improve, simply by traveling to work everyday on your bicycle. Hills that once seemed daunting will no longer be a challenge but just part of your trip to work. You'll start sleeping better, breathing better, your blood pressure will improve, your waist may shrink. Don't let your improving health diminish over the weekend. Weekends are made for bicycling. Get out there and explore your world. Pack a picnic and take your family on a biking excursion to a local park. Recruit a friend to bicycling. Join a local cycling club. Make a day trip to the country by bike.

Bicycles are inherently social vehicles. Commuting by car is an isolating experience, travel in a metal and glass chamber at highest possible velocity. Drivers are alienated from the neighborhoods they drive through; these communities are merely impediments in the motorist's way as they speed to their destination. When you commute by bicycle, you are immersed in the terrain. You are part of your environment. The neighborhoods you travel through offer delights and surprises. The slower pace of bicycle commuting means you can easily stop to smell the roses.

Don't be surprised if you start relating to people differently. They are no longer mere scenery seen through a windshield as a high-speed blur, but real individuals who wave to you. Expect more conversations, often started by a question about your bicycle. In short, bicycling is a social activity. There are many ways to extend your social engagement with the world through bicycling, including advocacy, recreation, touring, and racing.

ADVOCACY

Many motorists automatically join national or state automobile associations. They may join to get roadside assistance, maps, insurance, trip planning, or other services. But they are also supporting advocacy for automobiles. Bicyclists don't join bike advocacy organizations as automatically. This is a mistake. Conditions have gradually improved over the past two decades for bicyclists, thanks to the efforts of bicycle advocates at the local, state, and national level. Thanks to these efforts, we now enjoy more bike lanes, bike paths, bike parking, bike-friendly transit, bike education programs, and bike parking than ever before. Much remains to be done. As you become a bicycle commuter, consider supporting a bicycle advocacy organization, which is working to protect your rights and improve your experience on the streets. Join the League of American Bicyclists, and find a local organization working to improve your local streets.

For most of the late twentieth century, bicyclists were considered inferior road users in the United States. Bicycles were marginalized as children's toys and recreational devices, not as serious means of transportation. For too long, many government officials and traffic planners neglected bicycling, walking, and transit use, giving priority to automobile movement over everything else. Neighborhoods were destroyed to build freeways, historic buildings were demolished to create parking garages, natural areas were paved over to enhance automotive speed. However, there are many things more important than the velocity of automobiles, including sense of community, historic heritage, quiet streets, neighborhood quality of life, clean air, cultural vibrancy, economic vitality, and the safety of children, pedestrians, and senior citizens.

Happily, national transportation policy has slowly started to change. Starting with the growth of environmentalism in the 1970s and the oil shocks of that decade, bicyclists started to seriously organize to challenge their inferior position on public streets. Bicycle advocacy has grown significantly since, making many important achievements. Together with their allies in environmental organizations, historic preservation groups, and public health organizations, bicycle advocates won passage of the landmark Intermodal Surface Transportation Efficiency Act (ISTEA) in 1991. The first federal transportation reform in the post-Interstate Highway System era, ISTEA marked a major change to federal transportation planning and policy. ISTEA gave greater control on spending decisions to regional governments, and for the first time ever provided federal funding support for bicycle facilities. ISTEA expired in 1997, and was followed by the Transportation Equity Act for the 21st Century (TEA-21) in 1998, and by the Safe, Accountable, Flexible, Efficient Transportation Equity Act: A Legacy for Users (SAFETEA-LU) in 2005.

These landmark transportation bills have enabled significant increases in the spending of federal transportation dollars on bicycle and pedestrian projects. In the twenty years prior to ISTEA, an average of less than $2 million per year was spent on bicycle and pedestrian facilities by all 50 states combined. Since the passage of ISTEA, this amount has grown to more than $200 million per year, totaling more than $2.3 billion of federal funding invested in bicycling and walking since 1991. Clearly, compared to the support given to automobile travel, this is insufficient. But it's a clear and encouraging sign of progress. Advocacy is working for bicyclists.

WHAT YOU CAN DO TO HELP BICYCLE ADVOCACY
- Ride as often as you can; be a model and example.
- Join a local advocacy organization.

- Volunteer with a local advocacy organization.
- Write letters to local media supporting bicycling.
- Attend public hearings in support of bicycling.
- Find out about the laws and issues concerning bikes.
- Contact legislators and work with government agencies to improve bike safety.
- Vote for legislators that support bike safety measures.

GOALS OF BICYCLE ADVOCATES

- Improve bicycling facilities in all areas.
- Improve multimodal transit access.
- Improve bicycle parking, including valet parking facilities.
- Promote bicycling in media.
- Create bicycle-route networks.
- Promote safe bicycling for recreation and transportation.
- Demand bicycling safety education.
- Defend cyclists' rights to the roads.
- Raise awareness of bike safety.

SOME BICYCLE ISSUES THAT NEED ADVOCATES

- Make bicycle parking available at transit stations, airports, and government buildings.
- Legislation to require bike-commuter facilities, such as changing rooms and showers, in office buildings
- Legislation requiring cash equivalent of parking space to bicycle commuters
- Tax policy supporting nonmotorized transportation
- Create bicycle accommodations on trains, buses, and other public transportation.

- Improve bike access on public roads, including highways.
- Improve bike access to bridges and tunnels.
- Address bike access concerns in the planning of new roads.
- Gain access to trails and create new trails in state and national parks.

References

Ballantine, Richard and Richard Grant. *Richard's Ultimate Bicycle Book.* New York: Dorling Kindersley, 1992.

Bicycling Magazine, eds. *The Most Frequently Asked Questions about Bicycling.* Emmaus, PA: Bicycling Books, 1980.

Brown, Lester R. and Janet Larsen. "World Turning to Bicycle for Mobility and Exercise: Bicycle Sales Top 100 Million In 2000." Earth Policy Institute. Available at *http://www.earth-policy.org/Updates/Update13.htm*

Centers for Disease Control and Prevention. "Overweight and Obesity." Available at *http://www.cdc.gov/nccdphp/dnpa/obesity/*

Chauner, David and Michael Halstead. *Tour de France Complete Book of Cycling.* New York: Villard Books, 1990.

Drake, Geoff. "Do the Right Thing." *Bicycling Magazine.* February 1995.

Ford, Norman D. *Keep On Pedaling: The Complete Guide to Adult Bicycling.* Woodstock, VT: The Countryman Press, 1990.

Forester, John. *Effective Cycling.* 6th ed. Cambridge: MIT Press, 1993.

Glowacz, Dave. *Urban Bikers' Tricks & Tips: Low-Tech & No-Tech Ways to Find, Ride, & Keep a Bicycle.* Chicago: Wordspace Press, 2004.

Honig, Daniel. *How to Bike Better.* New York: Ballantine Books, 1985.

Landers, Daniel M. *The Influence of Exercise on Mental Health*. Arizona State University. Available at *http://www.fitness.gov/mentalhealth.htm*

LeMond, Greg and Kent Gordis. *Greg LeMond's Complete Book of Bicycling*. New York: G. P. Putnam's Sons, 1990.

Maryland Department of Transportation. "A Safety Handbook for Bicycle and Moped Owners." Revised 1995. Baltimore.

Matheny, Fred. *Bicycling Magazine's Complete Guide to Riding and Racing Techniques*. Emmaus, PA: Rodale Press, 1989.

Nye, Peter. *The Cyclist's Sourcebook*. New York: Perigee Books, 1991.

Panning, Jennifer C. "Mental Health Benefits of Exercise." FindCounseling.com *Mental Health Journal,* November 2000. Available at *http://www.findcounseling.com/journal/health-fitness/*

Perry, David B. *Bike Cult*. New York: Four Walls Eight Windows, 1995.

Rails to Trails Conservancy. "The Short Trip with Big Impacts: Walking, Biking and Climate Change." Available at *http://www.railtrails.org*

Roney, J. Matthew. *Bicycles Pedaling Into the Spotlight*. Earth Policy Institute. Available at *http://www.earthpolicy.org/Indicators/Bike/2008.htm*

Schwinn. "ATB Owner's Manual." Chicago: Schwinn Bicycle Company, 1998.

Staff of Bicycling Magazine. *Women's Cycling*. Emmaus, PA: Rodale Press, 1996.

Surface Transportation Policy Project. Transportation and Health. Available at *http://www.transact.org/library/factsheets/health.asp*

Van der Plas, Rob. *The Bicycle Commuting Book*. San Francisco: Bicycle Books, 1989.

Van der Plas, Rob. *Bicycle Technology*. San Francisco: Bicycle Books, 1991.

Weaver, Susan. *A Woman's Guide to Cycling*. Berkeley, CA: Ten Speed Press, 1991.

Woodyard, Chris. "AAA: Most costs of auto ownership rise this year," *USA Today,* March 27, 2007.

Glossary of Bicycling Terms

aerodynamics
The study of the motion of air and its influence on moving objects. Aerodynamic refers to the ability of an object to move through the air with the least wind resistance.

ATB
All-terrain bike, or mountain bike.

ball bearings
Small steel spheres in the joints of machines (including bicycles) to allow rotation of the parts.

BMX
Bicycle moto-cross.

bottom bracket
Point at which the seat tube and down tube connect; incorporates the axle for the crankset.

brake pads
Rubber pieces on the brakes that come in contact with the rim of the wheel to stop the bike.

braze-ons
Frame attachments, which have been secured through a heated metal brazing process, that hold objects such as air pumps, water bottles, and panniers.

butted frame
Bike frame on which tubes are thicker at the ends—where they connect with other tubes and bear the most stress—and thinner in the middle.

cadence
Number of revolutions per minute of a pedal.

caliper brakes
Common brake design using connected arms that squeeze around the outside rims of the wheel to stop the bike.

cantilever brakes
Brake design using individual brake pads on both sides of the rim, pulled by a lever to stop the bike.

carbon fiber
Lightweight material consisting of extremely thin fibers of carbon bonded together, used in construction of bicycle frames, forks, components.

cassette
Set of rear sprockets that attach to the hub on the rear wheel.

century
One hundred-mile bike ride or race (sometimes 100 kilometers, called a metric century).

chainwheel (chainring)
Sprockets held around the bottom bracket and turned by the cranks.

clincher tire
Common tire design in which the tire has beads that hook into the rim and is held in place by the pressure of the inflated innertube.

clipless pedals
Apparatus similar to a ski binding that connects a rider's shoes to the pedals without the use of toe clips.

coast
To ride without pedaling.

cog
Sprocket located around the rear wheel hub, connected to the chainwheel sprockets by the chain.

crankarms
Arms that hold the pedals and revolve around the bottom bracket to turn the crankset.

crankset
Mechanism consisting of the pedals, crankarms, chainwheels, and axle, located at the bottom bracket.

criterium
Multilap circuit race, typically held on a few city blocks.

Critical Mass
Large group bicycle events, held regularly to celebrate bicycling and/or protest automobile traffic.

cruiser
Type of bicycle with fat tires, comfortable geometry, and long sweptback handlebars.

derailleur
Mechanism operated by the shift levers that moves the chain between chainwheels in front or cogs in rear to change gears.

development
Distance a bike in a certain gear travels in one complete turn of the pedals.

diamond frame
Standard bike frame design in which the four main tubes form a diamond shape.

draft
To ride behind another vehicle (often another bicycle) to reduce wind resistance.

drivetrain
Propulsion mechanism of a bicycle, made up of the entire crankset, plus the chain, cogs, derailleurs, and shift levers.

drop handlebars
Handlebars with extensions that curve downward to enable a lower riding position.

dropouts
Slots located at the ends of the front fork and rear stays where the wheel axles attach.

echelon
Staggered group riding formation used to block wind resistance.

fender
Bike part sometimes found directly above the tire; used to keep water and mud sprayed by the wheels off the rider.

folding bike
Bicycle with a frame that folds for more compact storage and ease in carrying.

fork
Component that extends down from the head tube, then splits into two blades that connect to both sides of the front wheel; consists of a steering tube, or fork shaft, fork blades, and dropouts.

freewheel
Mechanism on the rear wheel hub that allows the wheel to continue turning forward while the drivetrain remains stationary or moves in reverse.

gear
Combination of one cog and one chainwheel turned together by the chain.

gear ratio
Ratio between the size of the chainwheel and the size of the cog in a particular gear; determines the development and pedaling difficulty.

headset
Head-tube mechanism that uses ball bearings to enable steering; an upper and lower headset are located at the top and bottom of the head tube.

head-tube angle
Angle formed by the top tube and the upper extension of the head tube.

high gear
Gear with a larger development and more difficulty pedaling; used for level ground and downhill.

honking
Riding out of the saddle; standing up while pedaling, for better acceleration.

hub
The centerpiece of a wheel that rotates around the axle and through which the spokes are threaded.

indexed gearing
Gear-shifting system in which shift levers click and derailleurs move the chain precisely into preset positions.

low gear
Gear with a smaller development and greater ease in pedaling; used for climbing hills.

lugs
Reinforced metal joints that strengthen the connections of tubes on the bike frame.

mountain bike
Bicycle with fat treaded tires and low gears, designed for use on a wide variety of terrains, including off-road and nonpaved surfaces.

ordinary bike
A high-wheeled bicycle common in the 1870s, also called a penny farthing.

paceline
A riding formation in which riders draft in line behind a leader.

pannier
Touring bag mounted on the sides of the rear and front wheels.

point-to-point race
Noncircuit race with separate start and finish lines.

quick release
Lever located on wheels, brakes, and seats that allows fast and easy adjustments without tools.

racing bike
Bicycle with thin tires and drop handlebars designed for racing.

rake
The amount of forward slope in the fork.

recumbent bike
Bicycle operated from a reclined position.

rim
Outer frame of a wheel that the tire is attached to.

road bike
Bicycle—such as a racing bike, touring bike, or sports bike—designed for use on paved surfaces.

road rash
Skin abrasion caused by a fall off a bicycle.

saddle
Bike seat.

safety bike
Modern diamond-frame chain-drive bike, introduced in the 1880s.

sag wagon
Motorized support vehicle accompanying a bike tour or race, often carrying supplies, equipment, and food.

seat post
Bar holding the saddle that slides into the seat tube.

seat-tube angle
Angle formed by the seat tube and the top tube.

spin
To pedal at a fast cadence.

spindle
Axle that attaches to the crankarms, located in the bottom bracket.

spokes
Network of thin metal rods that connect the rim to the hub on a bike wheel and support the wheel through tension.

stage race
Multiday bike race consisting of a string of point-to-point races.

stays
Thin tubes connected to the main tubes of the frame that connect the frame to the rear wheel, including seat stay and chain stay.

stem
Bicycle component that connects the steering tube to the handlebars.

stoker
Rear cyclist on a tandem.

suspension
Ability to absorb bumps and shock from the road.

tandem
Bicycle made for two riders.

time trial
Timed race.

toe clips
Frames or stirrups attached to the pedals that hold the rider's feet in place when pedaling.

touring bike
Bicycle with wide-ranging gears, designed to carry panniers on long-distance touring.

trail
Measure of steering geometry determined by the distance between a vertical line extended down from the wheel axle and a line extended from the steering tube to the ground.

true
Term describing a wheel that is perfectly flat and round, with spoke tension balanced throughout.

tubular tire
Tire that is sewn around an innertube and glued onto the rim, used primarily for racing; also called a sew-up tire.

wheelbase
Distance between front and rear wheel axles.

Index